THEMES IN CANADIAN SOCIAL HISTORY

Editor: Craig Heron

COLIN D. HOWELL

Blood, Sweat, and Cheers: Sport and the Making of Modern Canada

UNIVERSITY OF TORONTO PRESS
Toronto Buffalo London

© University of Toronto Press Incorporated 2001
Toronto Buffalo London
Printed in Canada

ISBN 0-8020-4466-2 (cloth)
ISBN 0-8020-8248-3 (paper)

Printed on acid-free paper

National Library of Canada Cataloguing in Publication Data

Howell, Colin D., 1944–
Blood, sweat and cheers : sport and the making of modern
Canada

(Themes in Canadian social history)
Includes bibliographical references and index.
ISBN 0-8020-4466-2 (bound)   ISBN 0-8020-8248-3 (pbk.)

1. Sports – Canada – History.   2. Sports – Canada –
History – 20th century.   3. Sports – Social aspects –
Canada – History.   I. Title.   II. Series.

GV585.H678 2001   796'.0971   C00-933162-x

University of Toronto Press acknowledges the financial assistance to its publishing program of the Canada Council for the
Arts and the Ontario Arts Council.

University of Toronto Press acknowledges the financial support
for its publishing activities of the Government of Canada
through the Book Publishing Industry Development Program
(BPIDP).

Contents

Acknowledgments

Although it has become something of a cliché for athletes to explain any individual sporting accomplishment as part of a larger team effort, that metaphor certainly applies to the writing of this book. Over the past two years since Craig Heron first invited me to undertake this project, a number of people have provided assistance, encouragement, support, critical commentary, and advice. I am especially indebted to Gerry Hallowell, a long-time friend, and now my editor once again. I feel particularly grateful that he enthusiastically took on this editorial assignment even though his retirement from University of Toronto Press was clearly beckoning.

I am also indebted to the Social Science and Humanities Research Council of Canada for supporting my various projects on sport in Canada over the past decade, and to the Senate Research Committee at Saint Mary's University for its continuing support of this research. At Saint Mary's as well, I have been fortunate to have the advice of so many able colleagues, among them Michael Vance, John Reid, Dick Twomey, Jim Morrison, Peter Twohig, and Chris Fletcher. Mike and Dick both read portions of the manuscript and provided critical comments and suggestions.

As I prepared this book, I tried out many of my ideas on my undergraduate students, and profited especially from the input of graduate students in both the history and

Atlantic Canada Studies programs at Saint Mary's. Although I thank all of them for their interest, special mention should be made of the assistance given me by Bill Miles, Dan Macdonald, Cindy Kiley, Stephanie McKinstry, Valerie Brideau, and Meghan Beaton. In addition, my secretary Marlene Singer was always ready to help whenever I needed assistance, and her cheerfulness would always bring me up when I was down.

Beyond Saint Mary's there were many people who helped me clarify my ideas and offered useful assistance. I am indebted to Gordon Macdonald for making available to me his vast knowledge of the Olympic Games, and to Mark Dyreson, Steve Pope, Nancy Bouchier, Shirley Tillotson, and Tina Loo for their advice and interest in my work. I owe a special debt of gratitude to Alan Metcalfe, my old high school phys ed teacher, whose work on Canadian sport history is the foundation on which this book is erected. Between glasses of wine and good conversation over a memorable weekend, Alan also read and made helpful comments on an early draft of the manuscript. I also wish to thank Don Morrow for his continuing support and inspiration. While I was preparing this manuscript a good friend and wonderful colleague in sport history, A.J. 'Sandy' Young, passed away. I hope this book doesn't disappoint my helpful colleagues, and that Sandy would have been proud of it. If it does disappoint, the fault is mine.

Finally, and most important of all, this project would never have been completed without the love and encouragement of my wife Sandi Galloway, who has always eagerly involved herself as my partner in anything I try to do, and who patiently listened and offered advice as I explained what I was attempting to accomplish. Life without sport and history would be rudderless; life without Sandi would be inconceivable.

BLOOD, SWEAT, AND CHEERS:
SPORT AND THE MAKING OF MODERN
CANADA

Introduction: The Field

Canadians today live in a highly commercialized global sport environment. Wayne Gretzky, Lorie Kane, Jacques Villeneuve, Larry Walker, Silken Laumann, Donovan Bailey, Mike Weir, Elvis Stojko, and other high-profile Canadian athletes compete with the world's best in their respective sports. The Olympic Games, the Pan-American and Commonwealth competitions, and the world championships in hockey, soccer, golf, baseball, basketball, figure skating, and track and field are closely followed events. Satellite broadcasts beam these competitions live into our living rooms, while images of elite competitors fill newspapers, magazines, and billboards. Highly skilled and recognizable international athletes, both male and female, command colossal salaries, and within the current cult of celebrity, receive the public adoration accorded to movie stars and rock idols.

A hundred years ago, sport in Canada was more localized and less commercialized. Only a handful of Canadian athletes – oarsman Ned Hanlan, weightlifter Louis Cyr, distance runner Tom Longboat, boxer Tommy Burns – had international reputations, and those who did usually performed in individual rather than team sports. Organized team sports such as football, lacrosse, baseball, hockey, and basketball were still in their infancy, though growing in popularity. The promoters of organized sport contended that sport cultivated both 'manly virtues' and a healthy nation. They regarded sport not simply as pleasurable entertainment, but as an instrument for social and moral improvement and for nation building. In contrast, critics of sporting culture worried that rowdiness, gambling, commercialization, and the professionalization of play would sully these new urban amusements.

The revival of the modern Olympic Games near the end of the nineteenth century reflected some of the contradictions inherent in sportive nation building, and some of the realities of the sporting marketplace. The first modern Olympics, held in 1896, was a rather low-key, exclusive, male-only affair, in which most of the contestants were well-to-do amateur athletes from Europe and the United States. In Canada, there was little public interest in the Games until after the First World War. Although Canadian athletes began participating in the Games in 1900, the country did not officially enter a representative national team until 1908. Before that, Canadian participants – be they individuals or teams – had to make their own way to the Games. Some Canadians wore the colours of other countries, or represented their American colleges. At the Paris games in 1900, Canadian George Orton won a gold medal in the 2500 metre steeplechase for the United States. Four years later, Canadians won gold medals in golf, lacrosse, and the 56-pound-weight throw, yet they received few accolades at home. Women did not participate at all. Lingering concerns about women's supposed physical frailty, and invidious assumptions about the 'unfeminine' nature of female athletes, meant that Canadian women would not compete at the Games until 1928.

The early Olympics adhered to the amateur ideal, which was inspired by notions of the sporting 'gentleman.' Of course, identifying the 'true sportsman' as an amateur and a 'gentleman' meant embracing an exclusivity based on both class and gender. Working-class athletes did not usually have the time or the financial resources to participate in international competitions; and the veneration of the 'manly' athlete left little ideological space for women to demand an equal place in competitive sport. Canada's sporting culture at the turn of the century was thus predominately male and bourgeois in character. At the same time, it was not yet fully integrated into the emerging capitalist marketplace. Over time this would change. As the recent history of the Olympic movement and the growing corporate presence in sport of all kinds suggests, sport over the course of the twentieth century became increasingly commercialized, and more global in scope.

Yet the transformation of sporting life over the past century has involved much more than its connection to the marketplace and its widening international character. In Canada, sport has always been important in the construction of gender identities, in debates about the body, in the shaping of ethnic, racial, regional, and community allegiances, and in the structuring of relationships between generations. Sport in Canada has served many ends. As earlier sporting traditions tied to rural or village life – often involving the use and abuse of animals – gave way to the more organized team sports of the emerging cities and towns, Canada's transformation from a predominantly rural to an urban and industrial society was facilitated. At the same time, sport influenced class relations, promoted civic identity and pride, and added to the infrastructure of nationhood. In short, the history of sport in twentieth-century Canada is a story of class and gender formation, capitalist transformation, and nation building in the broadest sense.

Historians often disagree about how sport should be approached. And they always disagree on how to define it. Some take a rather inclusive view, arguing that any game, contest, or competitive leisure pursuit that involves physical activity ought to be designated as a sport. This would include recreational play as well as organized competitive games. Others distinguish sport from recreation, and focus their attention on formal, organized activities involving sporting clubs and associations. Modernization theorists analyse the changing structure of sporting practices over time. They contrast the fluid and unstructured sporting activities of traditional societies with the highly regularized, specialized, and codified modern sporting culture. For those historians who adhere to the modernization model, sport differs from recreation in the way it has bureaucratized itself, in the attention it pays to scheduling and rules making, in its preoccupation with record keeping and the statistical measurement of performance.

Another way of approaching the history of organized sport in Canada over the past century is as part of a larger process of economic and cultural production. The early promoters of sport in the nineteenth century who fenced grounds, built grandstands, and charged admission were well aware of how sport could be exploited for profit. As a commodity to be bought and sold, sport was ideal. Games are easily renewed resources: once one match has been completed, another can begin. The costs associated with producing a match are limited mainly to providing equipment for the players, renting the grounds, advertising the event, and paying the salaries of the athletes and support staff. The profitability of the enterprise is related to these expenses, and also to the range of choices in the wider leisure marketplace. So historians have been interested in how the sporting marketplace has developed over the past century – how it has, within our own time, expanded beyond the relatively local to acquire a national and international character.

Thinking of sport as a commodity brings us into contact with a number of important issues and raises a number of important questions. Sporting professionalism, which in Canada began in the nineteenth century, redefined athletics as work, and connected sport to the struggle between labour and capital that accompanied the development of industrial capitalism in the years between Confederation and the First World War. Professionalization also challenged the middle-class veneration of amateur athletics, which linked sport to character building and to traditions of fair play. Conflicts thus developed between those who promoted sport as a moral tonic, and those entrepreneurs and athletes who saw it as an opportunity for making money. So we might ask: how have assumptions about the appropriate balance between professional and amateur sport changed over time? Have sport's social purposes been undermined by its excessive commercialism? If sport is a commodity, what other purposes should it serve?

The debate about the social value of sport is ongoing. Some argue that sport is a form of 'social capital' that encourages civic improvement and loyalty to the community, and inculcates notions of fair play and social peace; others draw attention to its more negative characteristics. According to Varda Burstyn, sport at times promotes personal well-being, community solidarity, and social equality, but more often it supports and affirms 'an elitist, masculinist account of power and social relations.' Other critics contend that sport diverts attention from serious social issues, undermines critical sensibilities, and leads to a passive citizenry that readily accepts existing class and gender relations as natural.

And so, like sport itself, sport history is contested territory. Moreover, how we address the social significance of sport depends on which sport we are assessing. Think for a moment about the contested social meanings and values attached to sports as different as golf and boxing, synchronized swimming and hunting, cricket and ice hockey, curling and car racing, volleyball and football. For some, boxing is one of the 'manly arts,' suggesting both dedicated training in the skills of self-defence and the identification of masculinity with physical power. For others it is simply staged brutality, exploiting participants and audience alike in a theatre of senseless violence. Synchronized swimming offers up a similar paradox: on the one hand it is a marvellous demonstration of mastery of the body, but on the other it reinforces physical images of appropriate femininity and reproduces what Naomi Wolf calls the 'beauty myth.' And as a final example, take hunting, which can be understood in so many different ways: as a rite of passage in which young boys are transformed into men by shooting their first bird, squirrel, or deer; as a necessary form of subsistence for those who make their life from the land; as a personal act of getting in touch with nature; or as an exercise of senseless destruction. In each case, the meaning of sport is open to interpretation.

Whatever their different assumptions about sport's value might be, sport historians of all persuasions must always address two fundamental questions. What is sport? And what is it for? The answers to these questions are not as simple as one might think. In the pages that follow we will look at the transition from rural to urban sport; the impact of sport on the debate about respectable behaviour at the turn of the last century; the lure of money and fame; the shifting discourses about fitness and the body; the implications sport has had for the construction of gender, racial, ethnic, and civic identities; and the connection between sport and nation building. And we will consider how elite athletics has been absorbed into an emerging global sporting culture. This history of blood, sweat, and cheers is thus a story of the making of Canada through sport. Let the game begin!

1

Blood

Between Confederation and the First World War, Canada underwent a profound social, economic, and intellectual transformation as it began developing into a modern industrial capitalist state. Under the leadership of Prime Minister John A. Macdonald, the political and economic infrastructure of the new nation was put in place. Macdonald's 'national policy' – tariff protection for Canadian industry, prairie settlement, and the building of a transcontinental railway to stitch the nation together – became the country's broadly accepted development strategy. By the First World War, Manitoba, British Columbia, Prince Edward Island, Saskatchewan, and Alberta had joined with Ontario, Quebec, New Brunswick, and Nova Scotia to create a nation of continental proportions. As waves of new immigrants settled the prairies, and urban industrial centres expanded, sport in Canada played an important role in asserting new conceptions of citizenship and negotiating the transition from a preindustrial economy to a rapidly growing urban and industrial order.

The sporting culture that developed in these years was tied to the development of Canada's cities and towns. Urban sporting activities differed from those that predominated in the countryside. Rural sport often involved animals, and interaction with the natural environment or wilderness. Hunting, fishing, canoeing, swimming, snowshoeing, skating, cockfighting, rifle competitions, and wrestling were popular pastimes, and holidays were often the occasion for greasy pig chases, scrub horse races, and slippery pole climbing. Games were fluid in structure, informal in their presentation, loosely organized, and irregularly scheduled. Sport in the countryside reflected the rhythms of agricultural production and the proximity of human beings and animals, rather than the factory whistle, the time clock, and the shop floor.

In the nation's towns and cities, new forms of industrial production meant a sharper distinction than before between work and leisure time. Sporting activities had to conform to the leisure hours available to athletes and spectators alike. The scheduling of games and the reporting of their location by the local press reflected new attitudes about organizing time. In the same vein, the organized sporting culture of urban society reflected limitations of space. In the countryside, sporting activities often took place in open and unbounded spaces; in urban centres, space was at a premium, and clearly demarcated playing grounds emerged for the various team sports. In the cities, sport reformers and businessmen attacked undisciplined street play as a threat to public order and commercial prosperity, and championed amateur athletic associations or private clubs as the appropriate venues for 'respectable' sport. The new urban sporting culture thus conformed to the spatial and temporal requirements of the urban and industrial landscape, and to bourgeois assumptions about respectable leisure.

There was limited tolerance for unsupervised street play in the nineteenth-century 'walking city'; there was even less tolerance for the keeping of animals. As Bettina Bradbury has shown, sanitary reformers in Montreal attacked the keeping of pigs – one of the survival strategies of the working poor – on the grounds that it endangered public health. This assault on the keeping of animals in urban centres would eventually extend to cows and horses.

In addition, reformers from organizations such as the Society for the Prevention of Cruelty to Animals (SPCA) decried the brutality to animals that was central to 'blood' sports such as cockfighting and bear, rat, and dog baiting. In the cities, new forms of organized sporting activity, including team sports such as baseball, lacrosse, hockey, basketball, and football, emerged to supplant or modify those traditional preindustrial sporting activities which involved close association between humans and animals. It is worth noting, however, that the organized sporting culture that developed alongside the new industrial capitalist order would never completely extinguish sporting practices such as hunting, fishing, horse racing, rodeo, mountaineering, sailing, canoeing, and various aboriginal games. These pastimes were rooted in preindustrial or rural life but avoided the worst excesses of blood sports.

Blood Sport

The impulse to reform sport had its source in the emerging urban bourgeoisie who adhered to Victorian notions of respectability. In Britain, attacks on traditional forms of recreation had begun even before the Industrial Revolution, and focused mainly on activities involving cruelty to animals. Bear and bull baiting, dog fights, cockfighting, ratting, and other blood sports were attacked as un-Christian and – because they were accompanied by gambling and alcohol consumption – written off as disreputable and irrational diversions from responsibility and honest labour. In Canada, governments at all levels passed laws against these activities and began licensing saloons, bowling alleys, billiard rooms, and roller rinks. By 1870 the federal government had banned blood sports, animal baits, and prizefighting. Even though they were now illegal, these activities persisted well into the twentieth century. Indeed, in some quarters there was considerable resistance to the bourgeoisie's concept of respectable athleticism.

The struggle to redefine recreation was particularly intense in working-class taverns. For much of the nineteenth century, taverns, saloons, and drinking shanties provided not only liquor but also a place to sing sporting songs, play billiards, and partake in other forms of sporting entertainment. Wrestling matches, prize fights, contests of strength, and activities involving animals provided patrons with a chance to gamble while being entertained. For example, at Joe Beef's Canteen in dockside Montreal, proprietor Charles McKiernan kept a menagerie that included at various times a tiger, a buffalo, and an assortment of wildcats, monkeys, parrots, dogs, and bears. The main attraction was Jenny the Bear, who sat at the bar with her cub, Tom, and regularly consumed twenty glasses of beer over the course of an evening. Black Daniel's shanty in Halifax had a pit for cock and dog fights; so did the notorious New York City tavern, where a scurvy fellow called 'Jack the Rat' bit the heads off mice for a dime and decapitated rats for a quarter. Bloody contests involving men and animals were by no means confined to taverns. In December 1879, the Guelph *Mercury* reported on a forty-five minute fight to the death involving pugilist Patsy Brennan and a Siberian bloodhound for a $250 prize. Brennan finally killed the dog despite severe lacerations to his arms and shoulders. More than a decade later, the SPCA in Halifax investigated a similar contest involving a man and dog in a barn behind a Creighton Street house. The provincial society continued to receive complaints throughout the 1890s about bears being exhibited and pelted with stones on the streets of Halifax and Amherst.

Not surprisingly, these activities offended the 'respectable' bourgeoisie and fuelled the campaign against rough recreation. What sport was there after all in bloody contests of destruction? Yet more than sport was at issue. At the turn of the century, Canadians were fascinated by the lines of demarcation between the 'civilized' and 'savage,' the 'normal' and the 'degenerate,' the virtuous and the vicious, the human and the beastly. For example, circus animals were trained to perform human activities such as riding bicycles, walking on their hind legs, and jumping through hoops; while sideshow tents featured 'freaks,' whose physical deformities suggested atavistic or animal-like characteristics. Ironically, institutionalized settings such as circuses and zoological gardens masked and legitimized the maltreatment of animals (and human beings for that matter), at the very time that reformers were attacking traditional sports such as cockfighting.

As blood sports came under the derisive gaze of turn-of-the century sport reformers, defenders of traditional recreations presented their own definitions of 'sportsman.' For example, promoters of cockfighting pointed to the activity's ancient lineage and its importance in developing improved breeds. The memorandum book of one cocker, Charles Wesley Dickinson of Brockville, Ontario, reveals that cockfighting had its own rules of etiquette and proper procedure. In this book, which he kept from before Confederation to after the turn of the century, Dickinson included articles of agreement drawn up by participants, references to the social composition of the cocking fraternity, and descriptions of the care he took in raising and grooming his birds. Dickinson was not one to throw a bird into the ring unprepared, and applied 'modern' scientific techniques. In this sense, he stood at the threshold between traditional and violent blood sports. According to Barbara Pinto-Green, Dickinson's 'opinions concerning animal cruelty, the value of scientific training techniques, and the importance of winning were not unlike those of the modern sportsman despite his illicit behaviour as a cocker.' However, cockfighting faced legal constraints and a middle-class assault on its respectability and would become a marginalized activity in Canada by the time of the First World War.

Hunting and Fishing

At the very time that blood sports were under assault, hunting in Canada was being transformed from a means of subsistence into a leisure activity that used the language of sport to justify itself. There had always been tension between those who hunted for subsistence and those who hunted for pleasure. In Britain, recreational hunting was linked to the aristocracy and its ownership of the land, and commoners often faced fines, imprisonment, or transportation to Australia for poaching on royal game reserves. In Canada, hunting had always been possible for anyone able to travel into the woods; however, the discourses that emerged around hunting in the nineteenth century were anything but egalitarian. Exclusive rod and gun clubs as well as fish and game protection societies proliferated in the nineteenth century, beginning with the Montreal Hunt Club (1828) and followed by others from Halifax to Victoria and most urban communities in between. These clubs catered to the Anglo-Saxon elite, and drew on British military and hunting lore that associated the sportsman hunter with the expansion of the Empire. These self-styled sporting gentlemen criticized those whom they considered inferior – especially native people and 'pot hunters' who hunted and fished to survive – for their supposedly irresponsible and wasteful assault on wildlife. While plinking away at game, sportsmen rationalized their activity by advocating a conservationist code. In the spirit of fair play and gentlemanly conduct, they argued, sport hunters and anglers should be committed to perpetuating game and conserving wildlife habitats.

Ken Cruikshank and Nancy Bouchier have demonstrated that attacks on pot hunting could take place even in a developing urban environment. In Hamilton's harbour, Burlington Bay, in the name of environmental protection, fishery inspectors sought to prohibit net fishing and spearfishing through the winter ice. In the dispute over how to exploit a shared environmental resource – the fishery of Hamilton Harbour – commercial fishers, farmers, and industrial workers actively resisted those 'sportsmen' whose desire it was to restrict the fishery of the bay only to angling. From the perspective of the 'sportsman' and environmentalist, angling was 'respectable' leisure, and a natural and healthy alternative to less wholesome forms of urban entertainment; thus it had a moral justification that superseded the interests of commerce. Sport fishermen attacked the use of jacklights, torchlights, spears, and guns, which they regarded as unsporting behaviour. During the 1890s in Hamilton, an organized movement to preserve traditional modes of fishing, including the use of spears, brought together those who fished to supplement their income or diet. That resistance, led by the Hamilton Spearman's Association, succeeded in protecting farmers, commercial fishers, and working people from those who wished to control the resource for their own purposes.

Elsewhere, however, traditional fishermen were not always able to defend themselves in this way. In his study of the emergence of a sport salmon fishery in Atlantic Canada, Bill Parenteau has shown how 'sportsmen' successfully used the language of conservation to displace Native fishers along the Miramichi and the north shore of the St Lawrence from their traditional fishery. Under the sportsman's code, anglers had to be aware of the habits of fish and game, and of the conditions under which they thrived. Exclusive salmon clubs, such as the aristocratic Restigouche Salmon Club with its $7,500 initiation fee, provided tens of thousands of dollars to the government in leasing fees, supported fish hatchery initiatives, and provided guards to protect rivers from poachers. In turn, the federal fishery department instituted regulations, including a prohibition on spear fishing and a system for licensing net fishers, that limited Native people's access to the resource. By the 1890s, Native people had been weaned away from their traditional dependence on the Atlantic salmon, and were increasingly entering the sport fishing industry as guides. Native people were thus no longer competitors in the fishery. Instead they were facilitating the Victorian sportsman's longing to encounter the 'wild' and the 'primitive.'

Ironically, while hunting and fishing were regarded as antidotes to the hectic demands of the modern urban and industrial order, sportsmen were reshaping nature to their own purposes. Patricia Jasen suggests that the craving for first-hand experiences of the wild led to nature itself becoming commercialized and offered up in tourist images, souvenirs, and holiday packages for hunters and fishermen. Just as the city was undergoing an industrial capitalist transformation, the countryside was being reimagined as a tourist haven or sportsman's patrimony. For those urbanites who could afford it, hunting and fishing promised to restore the vital energy lost to brain work. As the argument went, civilization took its toll on human beings, weakening the nervous system and contributing to muscular flabbiness. It was thought that a periodic return to one's 'natural' roots, and experiences involving the wild and the primitive, had therapeutic benefits for dissipated brain workers. This romanticization of wild nature also involved notions of cultural superiority. In contrasting the 'civilized' world and the 'primitive' wilderness, sport hunters took for granted the superiority of Euro-Canadian culture and the inferiority of Native peoples, who led 'primitive' lives.

Hunting was thought to replenish the lost energy of neurasthenic office workers; its benefits to the country's wildlife were harder to identify. Conservationists might talk of controlling and regulating the animal population, and ridding the countryside of vermin, but the reality was often quite different. Although the sportsman's code frowned on binge killings or the mass slaughter of animals, these activities were far from rare. Soon after Canada's West was settled, the bison, pronghorn, antelope, and duck populations declined precipitously as sport hunters – many of them Americans – flocked to hunting grounds armed with breech-loading rifles and pumpguns. Between 1900 and 1940 the duck population on the prairies fell from an estimated 170 million to 50 million, despite attempts by the state to regulate hunting through licensing provisions, seasonal prohibitions against the taking of birds, and other regulations.

Although hunting had a more drastic impact on wildlife than the various blood sports – at least in quantitative terms – it escaped outright prohibition. Why was this so? In the first place, hunters drew on aristocratic and gentlemanly traditions of the mother country, and represented themselves as inheritors of a medieval sporting code with chivalrous links to the nobility. Hunting also buttressed prevailing notions of a 'manly' society. Hunting was mainly a masculine pursuit; and the hunting grounds were a male preserve that provided turn-of-the-century Canadian men with an alternative to the women-oriented domestic sphere and what they regarded as a feminized culture. Hunting was defended as a noble and gentlemanly activity and as a rite of passage to manhood, whereas blood sports were regarded as the activity of the uncivilized and uncouth, who lacked respectability and true manliness. In addition, the adoption of a sporting code of conservation – later given legal force by the state – ensured that hunting and fishing for sport and pleasure would be regulated rather than banned.

Horseracing and Equestrian Competition

Given the close association between humans and animals that characterized rural life and the preindustrial cities, it is hardly surprising that horses and cattle have been an important part of Canada's sporting history since the eighteenth century. Indeed, as Alan Metcalfe observed, 'no corner of British North America was immune to the passion for the horse.' Informal races, arranged on an irregular basis by individuals and often undertaken for a money prize or wager, have always been held wherever the opportunity presented itself. Formal turf associations and organized races over racecourses date back to the late eighteenth century in Canada. By 1768 Nova Scotia governor William Campbell had built a racecourse on Halifax Common, which attracted exuberant and at times unruly crowds of spectators. Racecourses of this sort were often established as alternatives to the impromptu and dangerous races for wager that sometimes invaded the streets of towns. Indeed, as soon as it began in garrison towns such as Halifax, Saint John, Quebec City, and Kingston, Ontario, organized horseracing on established tracks received support from the military and commercial elite. The sport also profited from its connections to the sporting traditions of the royal family. Canada's premier thoroughbred race, the Queen's Plate, dates from 1860 and symbolizes the sport's connection to the monarchy.

Equally appealing for the horsing set was the money to be made through commercially run racetracks, on and off-track betting, and the breeding of horseflesh. By the last quarter of the nineteenth century, there were commercially operated racetracks everywhere in the country. By 1900 the country's largest racetracks, such as Woodbine in Toronto and the Blue Bonnets Raceway in Montreal, were attracting large crowds and turning substantial profits. Horsebreeding was equally profitable, although it required substantial capital investment. Joseph Seagram, an Ontario distiller, was the leading breeder of the nineteenth century, and turned his earlier business successes into a horseracing empire. His horses won fifteen Queen's Plate championships. Seagram's twentieth-century counterpart, investment broker E.P. Taylor, became one of the world's most influential breeders. Taylor's Northern Dancer won the 1964 Kentucky Derby and went on to sire many racing stallions. By the time Northern Dancer died in 1990, his stud fees were exceeding a million dollars per foal.

Outside the larger urban centres, and in agricultural areas, harness racing or trotting was often more popular than flat-track racing. In the last quarter of the nineteenth century, standardbred racing spread rapidly in western Ontario, Quebec, and the Maritimes. Because it lacked the patronage of the wealthy, standardbred trotting was often disparaged by supporters of thoroughbred racing, and allegations of corruption and uncontrolled gambling swirled around the sport in its early years. In 1878 the Maritime Trotting Association was formed to provide some control over the sport, and six years later a Canadian circuit of the United States National Trotting Association was established in Ontario and Quebec. According to Syd Wise, trotting horsemen at the time were 'incapable of organizing to protect themselves from "the predatory horde of outlaws" drawn to their tracks.' These concerns were gradually put to rest. The twentieth century saw a number of technological and organizational improvements that put harness racing in Canada on a more reputable footing. The use of mobile starting gates, photo-finish cameras, and artificial lighting for night racing all contributed to a more professional image for the sport; and the licensing of racing judges, race starters, and drivers ensured that capable people would be organizing meets. Out of this environment, a number of Canadian harness drivers went on to successful careers at the international level. Hervé Filion of Angers, Quebec and, Billy O'Donnell and Joe O'Brien of Alberton, Prince Edward Island – each of whom got his start on the smaller racing circuits in Quebec and the Maritimes – won over 20,000 races among them, with combined purses in excess of $100 million. All three have been inducted into both the United States Hall of Fame of the Trotter and the Canadian Horse Racing Hall of Fame.

Equestrian competition has also had a successful history in Canada, especially since the Second World War. Tied as it is to aristocratic notions of riding, equestrianism has always been regarded as a respectable sport. Also, it has always been open to both men and women riders. In 1953, Shirley Thomas of Ottawa became the first female rider on Canada's three-member international team. Later the same year she was the first woman to win international class honours at Madison Square Garden. Canada's greatest successes came in the following decade, when the Canadian team led by James Day won a gold medal at the Olympic Games in Mexico City. In the 1970s and 1980s, Canada would be led by Halifax-born Ian Millar, who was recognized as one of the world's most successful riders. Equally notable was Millar's mount, the incomparable Big Ben, who fearlessly took Millar's commands and performed with a mixture of power, grace, and authority seldom seen.

Stampedes and Rodeos

Horseracing and equestrian competition reflected the early influence of Great Britain on Canadian sporting life; rodeos and stampedes emerged out of the conditions of the North American frontier. The great popularity of Buffalo Bill's Wild West Show, established in 1882, led inexorably to the popularization of competitions involving trick riding, bronco busting, cattle roping, bull riding, and steer wrestling. In Canada, competitions that resembled rodeos were held at Fort Macleod as early as 1891. By the turn of the century, similar events were commonplace at various agricultural fairs throughout the West. Raymond, Alberta, hosted Canada's first official rodeo in 1903.

The most notable rodeo event in the country has long been the Calgary Stampede. First held in 1912, the Stampede was the brainchild of Guy Weadick, a promoter and trick roper of the touring Miller Brothers Wild West Show, who convinced four Alberta businessmen to put up $100,000 to stage the event. A $20,000 prize purse attracted cowboys to Calgary from across North America and as far away as Mexico. The star of the show was Canadian Tom Three Persons, whose thrilling ride on a hitherto unridable horse named Cyclone made him an instant hero and $1,000 richer. In 1923, when the famous chuckwagon races were introduced, the Stampede attracted over 130,000 spectators. After the Second World War, the Stampede was placed on a more professional footing with the establishment of the Canadian Professional Rodeo Association. By 1990 over sixty professional rodeos were being held annually in Canada, and over $2 million in total prize money was on offer.

When folksinger Ian Tyson wrote a song expressing a young woman's lament that her 'parents cannot stand him 'cause he rides the rodeo,' he was alluding to the sport's aura of disreputability. He was also putting to music the gendered imagery that surrounds the myth of the cowboy. Rodeo has traditionally been regarded as a macho sport, as a male space within which there is no room for respectable women. According to Mary Lou LeCompte, it took considerable time for the women associated with these competitions to elevate themselves from 'chippies to athletes.' Yet women have always been involved in rodeo. At the first Calgary Stampede, cowgirls Florence LaDue, Lucille Mulhall, Fannie Sperry, and Canada's own Goldie St Clair competed in roping contests, bronc riding, trick riding, and relay races. Nevertheless, reporters tended to emphasize not the skills and technique of women performers, but rather their charm, beauty, personality, and domesticity, and their costumes.

Canoes, Boats, and Aquatic Sport

The sporting encounter with nature took many forms besides hunting and fishing. The nation's harbours, lakes, rivers, and beaches provided a venue for all manner of sporting and recreational activities. Boating, sailing, paddling, rowing, swimming, skating, and curling all had preindustrial origins. While originally undertaken as individual and spontaneous recreations, these activities eventually became more organized and competitive. Even without documentary evidence, one can readily imagine Native people racing each other in canoes or on snowshoes, and races between fur traders as they pushed into the hinterland. Boats, yachts, barges, dories, and even schooners could be turned into racing craft, and invariably were.

The presence of the British navy at various garrison towns provided particular encouragement for aquatic competitions. In Halifax, military regattas were held as early as the eighteenth century. In the years before Confederation, as they became regular events, they usually included barge and cutter races, as well as canoe races between Mi'kmaq paddlers. Native paddlers also participated in races on Rice Lake near Peterborough, and the Caughnawagas staged 'war canoe' races in conjunction with regattas held at the Grand Trunk Boating Club in Montreal. By the end of the nineteenth century, canoe and rowing clubs were flourishing in most cities, and rivalries such as the one in the nation's capital between the Ottawa Canoe Club and the Rideau Canoe Club created great interest in competitive canoeing. A graduate of the Rideau club, Francis Amyot, won a gold medal at the 1936 Olympic Games in Berlin.

By the early 1900s, rowing was even more popular than paddling, largely because of the success of Canadian rowers on the international scene. The triumph of the Paris Crew from Saint John, New Brunswick, over the best crews in the world at the Paris Exposition in 1867 briefly stirred the new nation's patriotism. In the 1870s and 1880s, Ontario's Ned Hanlan dominated the professional rowing world, further enhancing this sport's popularity. As Alan Metcalfe observed, Hanlan was one of Canada's most popular personalities at the turn of the century, rivalling Wilfrid Laurier in public recognition and adoration. Indeed, if Laurier foresaw the twentieth century as belonging to Canada, Hanlan's popularity suggested that it would also belong to sport. A world rowing champion for a number of years, and generally considered the first to master the sliding seat, Hanlan's races drew massive crowds. He retired from racing in 1901, but memories of his racing exploits did not fade. In 1926 a statue was erected on the Canadian National Exhibition grounds in Toronto to honour his memory.

Yet for those who adhered to Victorian assumptions of gentlemanly behaviour and venerated the amateur ideal, Hanlan's sport had a darker side. According to Bruce Kidd, Hanlan's career was at times characterized by crooked professionalism, the ducking of opponents, and the influence of the gambling set. Indeed, there was always a tension between the gentlemanly reputation of rowing as an amateur sport, rooted as it was in intercollegiate competitions between Oxford and Cambridge in England, and its rough-hewn and commercialized character as a popular sporting event in North America. Yet as Metcalfe suggests, the elitist contemporaries of Hanlan who criticized his desire to make money from rowing were often hypocritical. 'While glorifying the making of money by businessmen,' he wrote, 'they condemned the making of money in sport. This irony lay at the heart of sport in Canada.'

· As an aquatic sport, sailing avoided the commercialism associated with sports such as rowing, largely because it cost so much to purchase and maintain a yacht. Early sailing clubs, such as the midcentury Royal Canadian Yacht Club of Toronto and the Royal Halifax Yacht Club, were ambivalent about racing competition. Many of their members represented the social elite of their communities and felt that competition would turn a patrician pursuit toward unseemly commercialism. In her study of turn-of-the-century boating in the Thousand Islands region, Laurie Rush found a similar tension. Old-money families – many of them American sojourners from the northeast – used the area as a retreat, zealously defending their privacy and emulating the British gentry however they could. New-money families used boating as a means to demonstrate and enhance their social status, by competing for trophies and actively seeking publicity. Most yacht clubs were able to negotiate tensions of this kind, however. By the turn of the century, the most prominent clubs in the country, among them the Montreal Yacht Club (MYC), the Toronto Yacht Club (TYC), the Royal Nova Scotia Yacht Squadron (RNSYS), the Royal Hamilton Yacht Club (RHYC), and the Victoria Yacht Club (VYC), were all mixing competition, socializing, and a reverence for the Imperial connection in a broad celebration of class privilege and exclusivity.

In the twentieth century, competitive sailing gradually assumed an international dimension. This was especially true in the Maritimes, in British Columbia, and on the Great Lakes. On the west coast, sailors from Victoria and Vancouver competed with those from Seattle, Port Townshend, Tacoma, and Bellingham; while sailors on Lake Ontario from both sides of the border often accepted racing challenges. On the east coast, the 360 nautical mile race from Marblehead, Massachusetts, to Halifax was first contested in 1905. It is now run on a biennial basis, with over a hundred boats in five divisions. The connections between the Maritimes and New England were further consolidated after the First World War, when the schooner *Bluenose*, under the direction of Captain Angus Walters, established a reputation for speed on the open sea. Built in Lunenburg in 1921 to fish the Grand Banks, the *Bluenose* won the International Fisherman's Trophy Race seventeen times, and has established a secure place in national folklore. More recently, Canadian sailors have done well in Olympic competitions. In the 1980s, the Canadian yachts 'True North' and 'Canada II' took part in the America's Cup races. Halifax's Royal Nova Scotia Yacht Squadron served as the club of record for these vessels.

Canada's northern climate contributed to a number of winter sporting activities with roots in preindustrial life. Skating, skiing, sleigh riding and racing, tobogganing, snowshoeing, dog mushing, and curling were all suited to Canadian winters. Snowshoes, dogsleds, and horse-drawn sleighs were all important modes of transportation in rural areas and the North, and like the toboggan could easily be used for enjoyment as well. In cities there was a tendency to institutionalize these traditional leisure pursuits and nowhere was this more evident than in Montreal. The earliest organized sporting club in the country was the Montreal Curling Club, established in 1807. The Montreal Snowshoe Club was organized in 1843, and under its auspices snowshoe races were held in the city every year into the post-Confederation era. The Montreal Toboggan Club dates from 1880. The popularity of skating on ponds and lakes led to the establishment of skating clubs, such as Montreal's Victoria Skating Club (1862), and to the construction of skating rinks in Canada's major centres. The first covered skating rinks were built in the late 1850s (one of the earliest being in Montreal's St-Antoine's ward); by the end of the 1860s they were commonplace. It is important to note that in Montreal, sporting facilities and clubs were concentrated in English-speaking wards. According to Metcalfe, before the turn of the century organized recreation in Montreal was 'created by the English, for the English and played by the English Canadians.'

Transported from the countryside into an urban setting, these traditional sports would be transformed by industrial capitalism. Allen Guttmann's typology of 'modern' sport applies here. In an urban context these sports were increasingly characterized by bureaucratic organization, by the standardization and codification of rules of competition, by greater attention to scheduling, by more refined systems of measuring performance, by the application of scientific techniques to the improvement of athletic skills, and by a new emphasis on record keeping. At the same time, as sport prospered in the more regulated and confined urban sporting landscape, traditional leisure practices increasingly fell under the influence of capitalist promoters, who regarded sport as a potential source of profit. At times, such as in the opening of privately owned ski hills and lodges, commercialization intruded into the countryside as well.

Aboriginal Games

For Canada's Aboriginal peoples, sports and games have always been connected to the natural environment and have been relatively immune from market influences, although this is less so in modern times. Besides the ubiquitous games of chance, Native peoples traditionally engaged in various competitions that helped refine important life skills. Foot racing, spear throwing, horse racing, and archery contests all honed their hunting prowess. Among the Inuit, bouts of finger or lip pulling and other feats of endurance placed a premium on the ability to withstand pain. In Native communities, physical competition also served as means of resolving disputes. Chipewyan males wrestled to secure property that was in dispute, or to win a wife; in Inuit communities, showing one's ability to withstand the blow of an opponent without defending oneself settled grievances.

Stick and ball games were extremely popular among Aboriginal peoples, and were often linked to religious ceremonies. Lacrosse or baggataway, a Native game played across North America but most prevalent on the Pacific coast and in eastern Canada, was thought to exert control over supernatural forces and to heal sickness. It also strengthened the existing tribal leadership while promoting future leaders, and fostered a group cohesiveness that served the economic and military interests of the tribe. By the early nineteenth century, the proficiency of the Caughnawaga peoples at this sport was well known, and contributed to the popularity of the game among the non-Native population. There were many other stick and ball games, however. On the prairies, a game resembling shinny was played with a leather ball and stick. On the east coast, the Mi'kmaq and Maliseet peoples played a game called 'old fashion,' which resembled the British game of rounders. In the North, the Inuit peoples continue even today to play *anaulataq*, a kind of Inuit baseball, at their spring and summer hunting camps. Like many Native peoples in Canada, the Inuit are caught between two different ways of life: one associated with a traditional, seminomadic, and land-based economy, and the other emerging out of the cash-based and sedentary society of contemporary towns. In Inuit communities today, traditional and modern sports coexist, just as two different modes of economic and cultural production interact. When on the land in the hunting camps, *anaulataq* is the Inuit game of choice. In the towns, where achievement is more often understood in monetary terms, it is not *anaulataq* but ice hockey that has gained ascendency.

Conclusion

Over the years, the sporting traditions associated with rural life in a preindustrial society gave way to a more highly organized sporting culture. In part this was a result of the substantial demographic changes that accompanied the Industrial Revolution and the rise of cities. The new forms of sporting activity that emerged in the cities and towns across the country were associated with new systems of thought and production that increasingly brought leisure itself under the influence of the market economy. The capitalist revolution, as it extended beyond the economic sphere, raised ethical and moral questions that touched civil practices of all kinds, including sport. These moral concerns went deeper than the assault on blood sports and the legitimizing of other sporting activities that had roots in preindustrial life. As we shall see in the chapters that follow, debates about sport in the new nation of Canada addressed questions about respectability and reform, degeneracy and regeneration, propriety and social justice, patriotism and social responsibility. Yet the meaning of those words in a society riven by class, gender, racial, ethnic, and regional divisions was always in question.

2

Respectability

As the twentieth century opened, Canadian sporting life was still largely rural. In the countryside, sport was loosely organized and recreational in character, and involved an intimate connection to animals and to the natural environment. In searching for the roots of modern mass sporting culture, historians have sometimes overemphasized the extent to which organized sport had supplanted traditional sporting activities in late-nineteenth-century Canada. It is nonetheless true that in the larger urban centres and even the small towns, an organized sporting culture was emerging that conformed to the requirements of the industrial capitalist order. Under the watchful eye of an emerging Anglo-Saxon bourgeoisie, sport became a social technology employed to create a 'respectable' social order and a deeper allegiance to nation and Empire. Of course, to talk of respectable sport was to imply that rowdyism existed, just as to speak of the reputable was to acknowledge the disreputable. In Canada, 'respectable' sports were more likely to involve men rather than women; the English rather than the French, whites rather than Blacks and Native people, Protestants rather than Catholics, and middle- rather than working-class athletes.

British Sporting Traditions

The organized, urban-based sporting culture that emerged

in post-Confederation Canada had its roots in Britain. Many commentators have emphasized the important role the mother country played in the development of sport throughout the Empire. Besides field sports, British sports and games such as football, cricket, rugby, golf, tennis, and curling made their way to Canada with the early settlers. Officers at military garrisons found that sport improved the fitness and morale of the troops; headmasters introduced British games in private schools as a way of promoting physical hardiness and fair play; and at Hudson's Bay Company trading posts, football was organized for employees as a reward for good behaviour. In some parts of the country, especially in rural Ontario and on Cape Breton, Caledonian or Highland games were held as a means for recent Scottish immigrants to cultivate their links to the Old World. Growing out of the Caledonian societies, whose purpose was to maintain the manners and customs of Scotland, these games replanted 'tartan' athletic traditions such as the hammer throw and the caber toss in a New World setting – and sometimes invented those traditions outright.

Whatever their origins, these British games strengthened Canadians' connections with the Old World, by offering up ritualistic expressions of imperial allegiance and dominance. The Victoria Day and Dominion Day celebrations marked the beginning of the spring and summer sporting seasons respectively, and sporting contests were invariably a major part of the festivities. As Nancy Bouchier has observed, these civic rituals said much about the values of the community: 'Since community members organized the holidays for themselves ... they are a kind of public manifesto, with verbal and ritual texts.' In Victoria, British Columbia – a city that imagined itself 'a bit of old England' – baseball games and rowing regattas at the Gorge were standard fare on the Queen's birthday. According to James Merton, these celebrations replicated and reinforced the existing social structure. On the committee barge, separated from and elevated above the rowers and other spectators (many of whom were Native people, Asians, or British sailors), sat city officials, politicians, other members of the city's Anglo elite, and the lieutenant-governor.

Given that most sports had British or Canadian roots, holiday sporting competitions served to confirm and legitimize the Anglo-Canadian bourgeois hegemony. Victoria Day and Dominion Day celebrations varied little across the country, whether in larger cities like Victoria, Calgary, and Winnipeg or in smaller towns like Woodstock, Ontario, and Fredericton, New Brunswick. This suggests that few English-speaking Canadians drew any sharp distinction between Canadian and imperial allegiance. Team games, track and field events, aquatic competitions – if suitable water was nearby – and horseraces were often held. It was believed that sports and games promoted gentlemanly behaviour, individualism, social responsibility, imperial allegiance, and respect for private property, and helped win the consent of Aboriginal and immigrant groups to the new national order. According to Donald Wetherell, sport was an important means for instilling British values in Albertans, many of whom were recent immigrants from eastern Europe. He adds that because the process of inculcating values involved 'patterning' rather than 'direct imposition,' the history of sport on the prairies serves as 'a telling example of the working of hegemony.' In contrast, francophone Quebec seems to have been indifferent to British sporting traditions (though it must be said that research on sporting life in French Canada, and the social purposes it served there, is still in its infancy).

The new sporting culture that developed in Canada between Confederation and the First World War was dominated by team sports. The earliest of these, cricket, soccer, and rugby, were well established before Confederation; gradually they gave way to newer sports such as baseball, lacrosse, hockey, basketball, and Canadian football. For the most part, these sports were organized and promoted by middle-class urbanites with the intention of providing healthful recreation, counteracting the sedentary character of modern city life, and promoting 'manly' character and patriotic sentiment. Team sports were considered more effective than individual sports in promoting fair play, physical hardiness, physical and mental well-being, courage, endurance, teamwork, efficiency, self-restraint, innovation, competitiveness, and respect for others. All of these qualities were perceived as essential characteristics of leadership in the new industrial age.

Middle-class proselytizers of the sporting ethic, sometimes described as 'moral entrepreneurs,' were drawn from various walks of life. Churchmen, educators, journalists, social workers, merchants, engineers, doctors, and even novelists were in the forefront of the movement to create an organized sporting culture. In private schools and universities at the turn of the century, the preferred sports were cricket, soccer, and rugby, which were associated with British public school sporting traditions. Private school headmasters in Canada, most of whom were transplanted Britons, considered public school athleticism an essential component in both the making of 'gentlemen' and the progress of the Empire. In their minds, Britain's success in the world and her ascendency over the 'lesser races' were both connected to her status as the premier sporting nation of the world. Yet according to historian J.A. Mangan, British public school education before the First World War was characterized by brutality and militarism. All Canadian private schools of that era, including King's College and Rothesay in the Maritimes, Trinity, Ridley, and Upper and Lower Canada Colleges in central Canada, St John's in Manitoba, and St Michael's, Shawinigan, and Vernon in British Columbia, emulated British public school traditions. Most often they required their students to participate in 'manly' sports with the goal of building character and developing future leadership. According to Jean Barman, in British Columbia's private schools the 'relationship between character and leadership was pointed out time and time again.' In this environment, endurance and toughness fashioned on the field of play, and the ability to endure physical hardship and spartan living conditions, were prized as much as literary and mathematical skills.

Muscular Christianity

The mainline Protestant churches also preached the virtues of physicality. Near the end of the nineteenth century the doctrine of 'muscular Christianity' gradually replaced more pietistic and spiritual religious traditions, presenting an image of Christ as robust and manly. According to Billy Sunday, the American professional baseball player turned preacher, Christ was 'no dough-faced lick-spittle proposition, but the greatest scrapper that ever lived.' Using analogies involving the body, he called for a Christianity of sinew, bone, and muscle, rather than 'off-handed, flabby-cheeked, brittle boned, weak kneed, thin-skinned, pliable, plastic, spineless, effeminate and ossified 3-carat Christianity.' In Canada, notions of Christian manliness drew heavily on the writings of Englishman Thomas Hughes, the author of *Tom Brown's Schooldays* (1857) and *Tom Brown at Oxford* (1861). Hughes idealized public school sturdiness and Christian manliness. He called on young men to celebrate a vigorously human Christ and to practise humane Christianity through active, athletic, and morally upright lives. In Canada, the leading literary proponent of Christian muscularity was the Presbyterian minister and novelist Charles William Gordon, who wrote under the pseudonym Ralph Connor. National and imperial greatness, Connor contended, grew out of physical toughness and Christian humility. An advocate of the 'social gospel,' according to which Christianity was a force for building the good society, Connor believed that the nation's future depended on the moulding of men of good character. 'For not wealth, not enterprise, not energy, can build a nation into sure greatness,' he wrote in an unselfconscious celebration of patriarchy, 'but men, and only men with the fear of God in their hearts, and with no other.' Not surprisingly, Connor's heroes often were athletes, like the Princeton-educated divinity student in *The Sky Pilot* (1901), who wins the respect of ranch hands on the Alberta frontier through his abilities as a baseball player, and the Scottish immigrant and former international rugby star Allan Cameron, hero of *Corporal Cameron* (1912).

Canada's Protestant denominations attempted to win middle-class boys to the church by offering up a virile religion that was 'neither weak-eyed or maudlin.' Many churches established athletic teams for youth. Others established Boy's Brigades – an idea brought to Canada from Scotland in the 1890s. Capitalizing on the martial spirit of this period, and on what the *Presbyterian Witness* called the adolescent's 'natural love of militarism,' the Boy's Brigades employed military drill to mould Christian soldiers and promote exercise. In 1909, military drill was introduced into the school system after Donald Smith, Lord Strathcona, donated half a million dollars for that purpose. The Strathcona Trust influenced physical education in Canada's schools for decades after, linking exercise to moral and patriotic projects. According to Don Morrow, the new emphasis on military marching, rifle practice, and rigorous gymnastics was 'a giant step backward for child-centred education and for the introduction of sports and games into the curriculum. Instead of trying to educate the whole child, body and mind, the schools were set on disciplining the body and the will into military obedience.'

The Young Men's Christian Association (YMCA) was another organization that enshrined the principles of physical and moral training. The YMCA's fourfold plan – mental, physical, social, and religious development – was directed at middle-class teenagers from good families. The Y's athletic program focussed on gymnasium exercise and indoor ball games rather than the traditional field sports of cricket, rugby, and soccer, or newer games such as baseball and hockey. YMCA-sponsored summer camps usually featured swimming and hiking rather than baseball, which was considered lacking in demanding physical exercise. David McLeod's study of the YMCA and other character-building institutions of the day suggests that the reach of these organizations rarely extended beyond the middle class. Their objective was not to attract the poor and unwashed, but to protect 'respectable' adolescents from the temptations of tobacco, alcohol, and sex and from falling in with the 'wrong crowd.' According to McLeod, the social and athletic programs of the YMCA, the Boy's Brigades, and the Boy Scouts were 'directed against the bogy of the hooligan, against working-class loafers and shirkers, and against the possibility of lower middle-class boys joining the degenerate in their idleness.'

Basketball

In 1891 at a YMCA international training school in Springfield, Massachusetts, James Naismith, a native of Almonte, Ontario, invented the game of basketball. The Canadian origins of the game have become part of our national sporting folklore. After rejecting soccer and lacrosse as indoor games because of the likelihood of frequent injuries, Naismith nailed peach baskets to the balconies at two ends of a gym to serve as goals. Later refinements would give the game a modern look. A special basketball was developed to replace the soccer balls Naismith used. Backboards were added in 1893, and metal hoops in 1906. Basketball was an ideal game for the YMCA, whose sporting programs centred on the gymnasium and the pool. It provided a non-contact alternative to rougher field sports and provided competitive exercise to young men over the winter months. Having graduated in 1890 with a degree in theology from McGill – where he was a multisport athlete – Naismith embodied muscular Christianity. His comments to the first players, which included five Canadians, made his commitment to Christian respectability clear: 'If men will not be gentlemanly in their play, it is our place to encourage them to games that may be played by gentlemen in a manly way, and show them that science is superior to brute force with a disregard for the feelings of others.'

In the last decade of the nineteenth century, Naismith's game gained widespread popularity in schools, colleges, and YMCA gymnasiums across the United States and Canada. In 1892 basketball was introduced at YMCA gymnasiums in Montreal and St Stephen, New Brunswick, by two members of the original class in Springfield. By the turn of the century it was being played at many schools and amateur sporting clubs. Y-sponsored leagues were developed for businessmen, railway workers, and students, and interurban competition quickly developed. Unlike outdoor sports, basketball was largely insulated from violence and rowdy play, and its origins in the culture of Christian athleticism stimulated its rapid growth across the country.

Basketball's respectable image also explains its popularity as a sport for women. In 1902, Senda Berenson, director of physical education at Smith College, modified the rules of the game for women, to reduce the likelihood of physical contact and rough play. Berenson's rules restricted players to a particular part of the court, limited dribbling, and prohibited the snatching or batting of the ball from another's hands. Basketball quickly became the competitive sport of entry for most young women in Canada. In the decade before the First World War, women were becoming increasingly active in a number of competitive sports, including baseball and ice hockey, but it was in 'women's rules' basketball that they flourished. When Canada went to war, women's basketball grew in popularity, especially on college campuses. The most notable women's team of the day was the Edmonton Grads, established in 1915 and made up of students and graduates of the McDougall Commercial High School in Edmonton. Over the next two decades the Grads dominated women's basketball in Canada, winning every Canadian championship from 1923 to 1940, all twenty-seven games that coincided with the Olympic Games, and the Underwood Typewriter North American Championships for seventeen consecutive years. During their existence, the Grads won 502 of the 522 games they played. Kevin Wamsley notes that over the years the attention has tended to focus not on the women themselves, but on their winning record and the influence of their coach Percy Page: 'Implicit in this is the common understanding that having a man who was well respected in the community controlling all aspects of the team management was an important part of the social equation that facilitated the acceptance of sporting women as ambassadors of the city [of Edmonton].' In this sense, then, the idea of respectability in sporting life has even influenced how history has been written.

Lacrosse

Basketball was considered respectable because of its association with the YMCA and muscular Christianity. Lacrosse, baseball, and hockey all faced allegations of rowdyism and disreputability. In 1866, when negotiations leading to Confederation were in full gear, a Native team from the Caughnawaga reserve defeated the Montreal Lacrosse Club in the first Canadian championship lacrosse match. The match symbolized the sport's incorporation into a new, urban sporting culture and the coming of a new national order; it also underscored lacrosse's Amerindian origins. Alan Metcalfe has observed that historians can find most of the important themes surrounding the development of organized sport in Canada in lacrosse's early history. Among these are the strong influence of Montreal in the establishment of the new organized sport edifice, the continuing discourse about respectability and rowdiness that attached itself to the transition from amateurism to professionalism, and, given the pervasiveness of British and American cultural influence, the difficulty of establishing a uniquely Canadian sporting culture.

Before Confederation, lacrosse was almost exclusively a Native people's sport. The game had deep roots in Algonkian and Iroquoian culture, where it was played as a sacred ritual. By the 1830s, lacrosse was a fixture of life on the Caughnawaga reserve near Montreal and the St Regis reserve near Cornwall. Euro-Canadians' interest in the game developed at a sluggish pace. There had been a few Native exhibitions of lacrosse in Montreal, the first of them in 1834, and sporadic games involving both Caughnawaga and white players, including one at Montreal's so-called Olympic Games in 1844.

Organized lacrosse dates from 1856, when the Montreal Lacrosse Club was founded. After that year, the game experienced rapid growth in and around the city. In 1867, George Beers, a young Montreal dentist who had laid down a set of rules for the game in 1860, organized a meeting in Montreal to establish a national association and to adopt a uniform set of rules for the sport. The National Lacrosse Association grew out of that meeting, and Beers's rules were adopted as the universal rules of the game. By the early 1870s the game had a considerable following in and around Montreal and Kingston, and its popularity quickly engulfed Ontario and western Quebec. Lacrosse spread west to the prairies and east to the Maritimes in the 1880s, and gained substantial support in francophone areas of Quebec during the 1890s. However, outside Ontario and Quebec it failed to establish a lasting presence, except in Manitoba and British Columbia, where it was introduced to a degree into the school system.

According to Don Morrow, lacrosse was 'a major, perhaps *the* major popular team sport in Canada' by the mid-1880s; however, it failed to sustain its fan base. Alan Metcalfe attributes lacrosse's failure to emerge as a na-

tional sport like baseball and hockey to organizational problems, to its inability to achieve a compromise on the issue
of professionalism, and to continuing concerns about rowdyism and ungentlemanly play. The arguments over amateurism and professionalism were especially intense in lacrosse. On one side of the debate stood the Montreal Lacrosse Club, a staunch defender of amateurism and 'respectable' sport; on the other side stood the Montreal
Shamrocks, a group of spirited Irish Catholics from the
working class community of Griffintown along the Lachine
Canal, who placed a premium on winning and whose vigorous style of play at times bordered on the violent. Middle-
class commentators were inclined to exaggerate the
rowdiness of working class Irish Catholics. Fearful that the
diffusion of sport across the social spectrum would lead to
a breakdown of the social order, middle-class newspapers
like the *Montreal Star* often commented on the crude language and raucous behaviour of Shamrock supporters and
their team's ungentlemanly play. The class dimensions of
this discourse are obvious; the debate also reflected important changes in organized sporting life. According to
Metcalfe, Shamrock fans were the first 'modern-day sporting spectators' in the country, living and dying with their
team's fortunes. Both the team and its fans placed a premium on victory, and were willing to push the envelope of
respectable behaviour well beyond what bourgeois sportsmen considered appropriate.

Then there were the Caughnawagas, whose Native origins and playing proficiency were sufficient reason in most
eyes to deny them the status of amateur gentlemen. When
the National Lacrosse Association was reorganized in 1880
to become the National Amateur Lacrosse Association, the
Caughnawaga were excluded because of their professionalism. The treatment of Native lacrosse players was often
shabby and exploitative. As Frank Cosentino observes, their
superior skills were often emphasized in the hope of drawing spectators to the lacrosse field. At the same time,

'whether the Amerindian had ever played lacrosse or had in fact ever played any sport, he was declared to be outside amateur competition by virtue of having been born an Amerindian. Open competition, it was feared, would leave the sport bereft of gentlemen.'

Baseball Not Cricket

In the years between Confederation and the First World War, baseball established itself as Canada's summer sport of choice, pushing aside cricket and lacrosse. Because the game emerged out of a number of stick-and-ball games such as British 'rounders' and North American 'one old cat' or townball, it can't be established exactly where and when baseball was 'invented.' The myth that Abner Doubleday invented the game in Cooperstown, New York, in 1839 was long ago demolished. Credit has been given instead to Alexander Cartwright, a young New York bank clerk who wrote a constitution for the first organized baseball club, the Knickerbockers of New York, and set out rules for the game, which included the playing positions and the distances between bases. Canadian sport historians Nancy Bouchier and Robert Barney have suggested the game may have a Canadian origin, and refer to Dr Adam Ford's description of a game in Beachville, Ontario, in 1838, in a letter he wrote to *The Sporting Life* in 1886. In the long run, how baseball was invented is less important than how it developed. Given the various regional configurations of the game that existed before the mid-nineteenth century in both the United States and Canada, it is more useful to approach baseball's development as an evolutionary process.

What we can say for certain is that baseball grew rapidly everywhere in Canada in the third quarter of the nineteenth century. In the 1850s, baseball clubs in Ontario communities such as London and Woodstock followed the rules of the eleven-a-side Canadian game, while in the

Maritimes a New England version held sway. In Ontario around 1860, London, Hamilton, Toronto, Woodstock, and Guelph all adopted the Knickerbocker rules so that they could challenge baseball clubs south of the border. The standardization of the game's rules was virtually complete in Canada by the early 1870s. By that time teams in Halifax, Fredericton, and Saint John had abandoned the New England game. Baseball in Canada was becoming highly competitive and skilled. In 1874 the Guelph Maple Leafs won the world semiprofessional baseball championship. Two years later they joined the newly formed International Association, along with the London Tecumsehs. Baseball had also made substantial inroads in francophone Quebec.

Baseball's rapid growth was evident not only in Canada's largest urban centres, but in virtually every small town across the country, and came at the expense of both cricket and lacrosse. Cricket was never able to excite Canadians as it did colonists in most other parts of the empire; it would remain the pursuit of elite groups, the military, and recent immigrants. Lacrosse had a substantial presence in Ontario and Quebec but made only limited inroads into the Maritimes. David Cooper has recently applied a 'diffusion process' model to explain how cricket was rejected in Canada, even though it became a staple in the West Indies, India, Australia, and other British colonies. Diffusion theorists such as Allen Guttmann and John Bale contend that sports radiate from their point of origin (in cricket's case from England to her colonies), and then downward from the top of the social hierarchy. In addition, Richard Cashman has paid particular attention to how sports are adapted to meet local needs, and how they are assimilated into the dominant sporting culture of the nation. Cooper offers various reasons why the diffusion process for cricket was never completed in Canada: the exclusive, upper-class, Anglophile character of the game; the steadfast opposition to professionalization, which meant that the talents of English professional players and coaches were ignored; and the failure of Canadian cricketers to fare well in international matches. Victories against English, Australian, and American visitors might have stimulated nationalist sentiments, enhanced 'self-esteem,' and led to a broader public acceptance of cricket; instead, the Canadian record against international opposition between 1859 and 1960 was a dismal 49 wins and 227 losses.

If we reject the notion of downward diffusion, and take instead a 'bottom up' approach, a different explanation emerges. In an earlier study of baseball in the Maritimes, I argued that baseball's popularity and cricket's limited attraction was a function of baseball's incorporation into an emerging working-class culture. Although the game had originated as a game for youthful members of the advancing middle class, after 1870 baseball became predominantly a working-class sport, one that encouraged fraternal feelings among skilled workingmen. Bryan Palmer suggests that in Hamilton, baseball served – along with mechanics' festivals, parades, and union balls and picnics – to enhance working-class solidarity and to illuminate and dramatize class inequalities. This was also true in Saint John and Halifax (and no doubt in Montreal, Toronto, Winnipeg, and Vancouver), where teams such as the Shamrocks and the Resolutes carried the hopes of working people onto the field, and where games involving printers, shoemakers, and other tradesmen maintained a loyalty to the craft.

Cricket, on the other hand, was generally perceived to be a bourgeois game and a bastion of class privilege. Thus, when the Philadelphia Cricket Club visited Halifax in 1874, it received red carpet treatment from city officials and the social elite. Over the nine-day event the city offered up yachting parties, balls at Government House and at private mansions, dinners held by the mayor and by officers of the garrison, and lunches at private clubs and in regimental messes. No such treatment was ever accorded touring baseball clubs. Nancy Bouchier has found a similar exclusiveness in the sporting habits of the mid-century 'aristocrats' of Woodstock, Ontario. Besides playing cricket, members of the Woodstock elite often rode to the hunt, competed in steeplechases, and went on hunting parties. These activities asserted the importance of elite groups and consolidated their social hegemony. At cricket matches, the urban bourgeoisie and local small-town elites displayed their fashionability, and in so doing claimed an ascendancy over the social order. According to David Scobey, the bourgeois props of fashionability grew ever more elaborate in the mid-Victorian era. The plush coaches, uniformed servants, and thoroughbred horses of bourgeois sportsmen 'reflected a paradoxical ideal of sociability ... and "aristocratic" exclusiveness.' So too with cricket. It is thus hardly surprising that these elitist associations made the game less than attractive to working people. At the same time, cricket's British character was unappealing to French Canadians, who were far more likely to take up baseball and lacrosse. At the St-Jean-Baptiste Day celebrations in St-Hyacinthe during the 1870s, for example, baseball was the highlight of the day for the community's citizens, over 90 per cent of whom were francophones.

As baseball grew in popularity at cricket's expense, the respectability of the game was questioned by those who saw in it the influence of the United States and of an unruly working class culture. Concerns were expressed about rowdiness, gambling, thrown games, and the consumption of alcohol by fans and sometimes by the players themselves. When an attempt was made to form a ball club at the University of Toronto in 1885, W.A. Frost wrote to the *Varsity* to warn students of the disreputable people associated with the game, such as a local tavern keeper 'notorious for his love of baseball and his generosity in bailing out of prison disreputable characters.' It was not the game that bothered Frost, but rather its unsavoury clientele: 'The associations of the game are of the very lowest and most repugnant character. It has been degraded by Yankee professionalism until the name of baseball cannot fail to suggest a tobacco-chewing, loud-voiced, twang-nosed bar-tender, with a large diamond pin and elaborately oiled hair.' Over the next two decades, however, baseball would shed its reputation for violence and corruption. By the First World War, the game had been transformed in the public mind from a struggle between the rowdy and the respectable, into a commercialized mass entertainment with broad support across the social spectrum. Although Canadians still vociferously debated the virtues of amateur and professional sports, there was a growing acceptance of baseball in its professional form. As we will see later, professional teams in Victoria, Vancouver, Edmonton, Calgary, Winnipeg, Toronto, Saint John, and Montreal became formally associated with organized baseball in the United States in the years immediately before the Great War.

Hockey

Baseball suggested the triumph of an American game over the Canadian game of lacrosse and the British game of cricket; it was hockey that would emerge and endure as Canada's truly national pastime. The origins of hockey are disputed for whatever its origins are worth. It was argued for years that hockey originated in Montreal in March 1875, when students at McGill organized a game at the Victoria Skating Rink and established its rules. Although this is a convenient notion for those who assert that Montreal is 'the cradle of Canadian sport,' the limitations of the claim should be considered. The argument is that the Montreal game was the first recorded organized match in the country. However, the rules employed, referred to as the 'Halifax rules,' were brought to Montreal by Haligonian J.G.A. Creighton when he entered McGill in 1873, and the sticks used in the game were carved by Mi'kmaq craftsmen. This suggests an earlier incarnation of the game on the east

coast. Recently the town of Windsor, Nova Scotia, has made
a claim to be the birthplace of hockey, based on a reference in T.C. Haliburton to a game of hurley on ice being
played on a pond near Kings College School at the beginning of the nineteenth century. In fact, it is likely that
around the same time, games of this sort were played by
military personnel at garrisons in Halifax and Kingston,
Ontario. The Mi'kmaq also had a game involving a stick
and ball and skates. It is unlikely that we will ever deter-
mine the exact origins of hockey. Furthermore, as with
baseball, claims to invention aren't as important as how
the game developed.

However it originated, hockey grew rapidly as baseball
had done, and was Canada's winter sport of choice by the
1890s. The game was well entrenched in Montreal, Quebec City, Chicoutimi, Sherbrooke, Trois-Rivières, Toronto,
Kingston, Peterborough, Ottawa, Halifax, Dartmouth,
Windsor, Saint John, Bathurst, and Charlottetown in the
1880s, and spread west to the prairies and British Columbia in this decade as well. Various leagues were by then
emerging among universities and amateur athletic clubs.
Hockey grew especially quickly in Quebec, and established
deep loyalties among French Canadians, whose disregard
for British team sports was profound. In 1886, clubs in
Quebec City, Montreal, and Ottawa formed the Amateur
Hockey Association of Canada, which included two of the
fastest clubs in the country, the Montreal Victorias and the
Ottawa Silver Sevens. In 1890 the Ontario Hockey Association (OHA) was formed, which except for the National
Hockey League (NHL) was the most powerful hockey association in Canada before the Second World War.

Hockey in its early days acquired a reputation for violence and brutality. In part this was a product of the speed
of the game, the frequency of body contact, and the dangers associated with the hockey stick itself. In the heat of
the game, brawls on the ice and in the stands were not
uncommon, and fans were known to pelt the ice with refuse

when displeased by a referee's call. Newspaper accounts often reported on incidents of this sort and on the serious injuries and even deaths that occurred in hotly contested matches. In the discourses about respectability and rowdiness in hockey, the key problem was how to distinguish the manly athlete from the violent brute. Typically, the explanations for the violence associated with hockey had class connotations, especially as working people took up the sport. On one side of this sporting melodrama stood the hockey gentleman who played with 'ginger' but also with respect for his opponents, the referee, and the game; on the other side were those players 'without proper breeding' who were attracted to the game because it allowed them free rein to hack and maim. Even so, because hockey drew most of its players from the middle class – young businessmen, professionals, and university students and so on – and because it had secured the support of important members of the social hierarchy, the game was never seriously threatened by its critics.

In 1893, Canada's governor general, Lord Stanley, whose two sons played for the Rideau Hall Rebels in Ottawa, donated a trophy to the Montreal Victorias as the champion senior team in the country. The Stanley Cup, which has since become the Holy Grail of hockey in North America, legitimized the game as one worthy of royal patronage, and also encouraged hockey challenges from across the country. Over the next two decades, teams from Montreal, Ottawa, and Quebec City dominated the sport, but challenges came from as far away as Dawson City in the Yukon and Amherst, Nova Scotia, in the Maritimes. In the opening decade of the twentieth century, the game developed rapidly everywhere in Canada. In the Maritimes, teams in Nova Scotia, New Brunswick, and Prince Edward Island competed for the Starr Trophy, donated by one of the country's largest skate manufacturers. In Quebec and Ontario, the Eastern Canadian Amateur Hockey Association was established in 1907–8, and was the country's strongest circuit at the time. The National Hockey Association, the precursor of the National Hockey League was formed in 1909, with teams in Ontario and Quebec, including an entirely new, all-francophone team, les Canadiens du Montreal. On the west coast, the Pacific Coast Hockey Association was formed in 1911. Like baseball, hockey grew in popularity as it became increasingly professionalized.

In the years before the First World War, then, the team sports brought to Canada from the mother country and promoted as builders of character were gradually pushed to the margins as games with North American roots became more popular and professionalized. Cricket, soccer, and rugby maintained their particular constituencies throughout the years, but their growth was limited by class boundaries and regional associations. Thus, cricket was played throughout the country, but was almost entirely a preserve of the anglophone elite. Soccer was popular in Ontario and British Columbia but had little purchase in Quebec or the Maritimes. Of the Canadian sports, lacrosse showed some potential for crossing regional and class boundaries, but its development was stunted by the growing popularity of baseball. Among French-Canadians, the sports of choice were baseball in the summer and hockey in the winter. Dan Ziniuck links francophone interest in baseball to the out-migration of Quebeckers to New England, where they worked in the textile mills and shoe-making factories, and to the practice followed by emigré Quebeckers of sending their sons back for high school and seminary education. Along with their books and their minds, these returnees brought home their love of baseball. When winter came, they put away their bats and balls, laced on skates, and took to the ice. By the First World War, baseball and hockey were clearly ascendant as the most popular summer and winter sports, and could justly claim to be truly national in appeal. Both had support across the country in cities, small towns, and the countryside, including francophone Quebec, and had followings that crossed the social spectrum.

Rugby and Canadian Football

Of the British sports, rugby represents a rather unique case. Although the game maintained a strong following in British Columbia and the Maritimes, elsewhere it underwent a metamorphosis, gradually evolving into Canadian football. During the 1860s and 1870s there was considerable confusion surrounding rugby football codes in Britain, Canada, and the United States. Some sporting clubs in Canada, especially those whose membership included recent British immigrants, subscribed to English variants of the game. At the same time, however, football codes were being formulated in Canada and the United States that would eventually lead to a distinctive North American version of football, with slightly different rule codes north and south of the border. After the imperial garrison was withdrawn from Montreal in 1872, the North American game quickly took shape. In 1874, games between McGill and Harvard resulted in rule modifications; visits by the University of Toronto to the University of Michigan in 1879 resulted in still more. Even so, there was not yet a uniform code of rules accepted throughout Canada, nor would there be for some time. In 1898, J.C.M. Burnside proposed a comprehensive code of rules, which although not fully adopted until 1921, provided the foundation on which the distinctive game of Canadian football would be erected.

Around the turn of the century, provincial and national football organizations were established and a Canadian championship was inaugurated. At the intercollegiate level, the Canadian Intercollegiate Rugby Football Union (CIRFU) was founded in 1897, and schools began hiring coaches with experience in the American game. Also the provincial associations of Quebec and Ontario, both founded in the 1880s, merged into the Interprovincial Union in 1907. This was followed by a 'national' championship game involving the CIRFU and the Interprovincial Union, which was played every year until 1915, at which

point it was suspended in deference to the sacrifices demanded by the war. Canadian football received the stamp
of royal approval when Governor General Earl Grey donated a championship cup in 1909. Initially this cup was
directed explicitly toward amateur competition, and was
an eastern trophy. Toronto Varsity were the first winners
of the trophy, defeating Toronto Parkdale 26 to 6 before
3,800 fans. As the game expanded westward, winning the
Grey Cup came to symbolize Canadian football pre-eminence in both east and west. In 1921, Deacon White's
Edmonton club was the first western team to compete for
national laurels, losing 20 to 0 to the Toronto Argonauts
before 9,500 spectators. Along with the Stanley Cup, the
Grey Cup became an important symbol of sporting nationalism in Canada. It remains so even today.

Maritimers and British Columbians showed less interest
in the Canadian game. Both regions maintained a firm
allegiance to English rugby that endured till well after the
Second World War. On the east coast, rugby had a strong
presence in colleges and private schools before the turn of
the century, especially at Acadia, Dalhousie, the University
of New Brunswick, Rothesay Collegiate, King's College
School, and Pictou County Academy. The Wanderers Amateur Athletic Club in Halifax fielded its first rugby team in
1882, and drew heavily on young professionals who had
graduated from the region's universities. Miners from the
coalfields of Pictou County and Cape Breton, where the
British manly sports and Scottish traditions of labour mili-
tancy shaped working-class consciousness, were also attracted to the sport. Before the Second World War the
most successful rugby team in the region was Glace Bay's
Caledonia club, which was formed in 1906 as an interme-
diate league team, and graduated to senior league status
in 1911. Its greatest successes were between the wars under coach John McCarthy. Between 1927 and 1939 they
won the Maritime championship McCurdy Cup eight times,
as well as ten consecutive Eastern Canadian championships.

Only after the Second World War did rugby give way to Canadian football in the Maritimes, and even then the process was gradual. Robert Kossuth contends that the acceptance of Canadian football in the Maritimes grew out of the wartime experience – in particular, the introduction of football at Stadacona and Shearwater military bases in Halifax, and the 'interaction with the rest of the country' that accompanied the war effort. During the 1950s the region's universities and high schools gradually turned to the Canadian game as well, and in 1965 an intercollegiate football league was established in the Maritimes.

Conclusion

In the years between Confederation and the First World War, Canadians created a sporting culture consisting of organized team sports in cities and small towns across the country and more traditional leisure activities in rural areas. Although disreputable blood sports had largely disappeared, sporting activities with rural roots and those associated with both animals and the natural environment continued to attract leisure seekers. The countryside offered sporting holidays for hunters, anglers, skiers, boaters, canoeists, horseback riders, mountain climbers, and other sport enthusiasts, and provided a respite for city dwellers from the hectic pace of contemporary urban life. Sport in urban Canada bore the imprint of the rapid transition to modern industrial capitalism. In its more organized forms, urban-based sport emulated the values of regularity and efficiency that characterized the emerging processes of industrial production.

Over the same period, sport became enmeshed in the broader enterprise of constructing a 'respectable' and manly nation within the British Empire. The churches preached the virtues of muscular Christianity, and called for a commitment to physical hardiness, social responsibility, and selfless patriotism. Educators in private schools and universities promoted soccer, cricket, rugby, and to a lesser extent lacrosse with the goal of producing leaders from among the country's youth. Since Canada as a nation was defined largely by its connection to Great Britain, and given that Britain's strength as an empire was often attributed to her sporting prowess, middle-class anglophones drew on British sporting traditions, including the 'character building' team sports, as a way of fostering imperial and national allegiance.

The new sport culture was largely the creation of an urban middle class that saw sport as a means for fostering the principles of fair play and accommodating working people, recent immigrants, and others to their authority. Later, as sport crossed class, ethic, and racial boundaries, questions arose concerning how effective it actually was as an instrument of socialization and as a way of ensuring loyalty to imperial Britain. Historians who view sport as an instrument of bourgeois hegemony should recognize the extent of working-class and ethnic resistance to that authority. Also, those who promoted sport as a crucible for moulding values feared that sport would succumb to the lure of the dollar. As sport increasingly became a source of profit for promoters, gamblers, and the athletes themselves, questions about respectability gradually gave way to concerns about how amateur athletes could be protected from the lure of professionalism. Over time, sport would outgrow concerns about respectability and rowdyism. However, the debate over professionalism would continue to rage in the interwar years, as organized sport emerged as a dominant element in an increasingly commercialized popular culture.

3

Money

Earlier in this book we asked two fundamental questions: What is sport? And what is it for? Between Confederation and the First World War, people's definitions of sport and their interpretations of its value varied with their social situation, ethnic heritage, and place of origin. We can say in general that sport provided different forms of leisure activity to people in the countryside and the city, and that these activities conformed to the patterns of production that characterized urban and rural life. In the cities and small towns of the nation, a new, organized sporting culture based upon team sports supplanted earlier activities that were more intimately connected to the natural environment and to animals. In the countryside, sports and games offered local inhabitants a respite from work and a way of interacting with neighbours; they also catered to the whims of urban dwellers, who sought a temporary escape from the seemingly artificial and debilitating routines of city life.

As we have seen, urban sport and games in the new era of industrial capitalism emulated the regularity, efficiency, and more disciplined scheduling of time that accompanied new systems of factory production. In cities, sport became a social technology employed to reshape the existing order. For middle-class proselytizers of sport, competition on the sporting pitch within a system of appropriately

drafted rules offered immense social benefits. In particular, team sports – many of them British in origin – incul-
cated notions of respectability, fair play, and 'manly' character, and fortified loyalties to nation and Empire. Furthermore, reformers hoped that a 'democratic' field of
play, open to those who would play by gentlemen's rules,
would dissolve the class antagonisms that accompanied capitalist transformation, and help win the support of working
people to the new order.

This hope of extending bourgeois hegemony was never
realized. Working people, ethnic minorities, capitalist promoters, crooked speculators, gamblers, and others were
intent on making sport conform to their own particular
needs. No one group could ever make sport simply an
extension of its own will, however reasonable its vision
might be. The fostering of civic responsibility, the building
of character, the instilling of patriotism, the cultivating of
manners, and the training of future leaders were all worthy objectives to those sportsmen who embraced them,
but in society at large other motivations were in play, from
carefree hedonism at one extreme to making a profit at
the other. Because of the involvement of so many competing
groups in the making of Canadian sport, those who preached
the sporting gospel never succeeded in their project of regulating morality and exerting hegemonic control.

The sporting field in these years was more contested
than consensual, riven by deep class, gender, ethnic, and
racial tensions that had their roots in the social, regional,
and material inequalities of the time. It is important to
remember that when athletes came onto the field, they
did so not as idealized 'sportsmen' – note the gendered
use of the term – but as products of a larger culture or
group that had done much to shape their thought. The
competitors understood sport's meaning in their own context of time and place. They were part of the moral, intellectual, and material world in which they lived. Some historians have emphasized the importance of a youthful

'bachelor subculture' in constructing the male leisure world at the end of the nineteenth century. This bachelor set, made up of both single and betrothed men, rejected the Victorian cult of domesticity and the family circle, and sought out companionship with other men in saloons, pool halls, firehouses, fraternal societies, militia companies, and political organizations and, of course, on the sporting field. Youthful fraternalism helped compensate for the father's absence from the home in urban industrial capitalism. The separation of domestic and workplace production, the growing percentage of single adult males in the Canadian population, and the tendency of young men and women to seek out different amusements, all influenced the configuration of modern sporting life.

The rejection of a domesticated family environment, and the tendency of men and women to seek out different leisure activities, had its parallel among working-class men, whose culture resisted bourgeois control. According to Roy Rosenzweig, working people asserted their right to 'eight hours for what we will,' and rejected the guidance of employers and social reformers with their improving intentions. In the male working-class culture, sport served a different purpose than it did for the bourgeoisie. When workers took to the baseball diamond, the lacrosse field, or the rink, they were demonstrating masculine independence, respectability, and physical skill in their own way. They were doing so, moreover, at a time when artisanal skills were being devalued in the workplace and when employers committed to the principles of scientific management were seeking to extend their authority over their employees.

The new sporting culture of the late nineteenth century was connected to new forms of economic production, and was emerging at a time when existing class relations were constantly being renegotiated. For these reasons, it is important to investigate sport as an aspect of the emerging capitalist economy. This investigation can be undertaken from two vantage points. First, one can understand the development of sport from the perspective of those capitalist entrepreneurs who saw in leisure an opportunity for profit. These men were less interested in the notion of sport as a moral tonic than many of their middle-class associates – especially those who were committed to the amateur ideal – and regarded sport as a commodity to be bought and sold. Second, sport's connection to the marketplace needs to be understood from a working-class perspective. Workers often resisted reformers' attempts to inculcate moral values that would have consolidated bourgeois hegemony; they were also drawn to the system of playing for pay or buying tickets to sporting events as spectators. By accepting sport's connection to the marketplace, workers were contributing in fundamental ways to the building of the modern commercialized sporting edifice.

Sport for Workers

For capitalists, commercializing sport involved turning it into a commodity that could turn a profit. For workers who sold their athletic skills as professionals, games and play were reconstituted as work and the sporting venue became a workplace. Skill is the key element in a professional sporting system, for without it sporting events have little market value. Warren Goldstein has noted the rapidity of the transition from playing a game like baseball for fun and cameraderie, to 'playing for keeps' (i.e., to win). Playing 'for keeps' involved practising more in order to sharpen one's skills. It also involved the introduction of 'scientific' training techniques and the specialization of tasks. For athletes, playing for keeps ultimately meant playing for money as professionals; for capitalists, it meant playing for profit.

Profit-seeking owners wanted to hire the most skilled players for the least amount of money, and to keep them subservient to management's authority and bound to their clubs by contract. Professional athletes, on the other hand, wanted to sell their skills in a relatively uncontrolled free market, and often resisted the control of owners by jumping contracts, boycotting teams, and developing players' associations that would bargain for them collectively. Of course, professionalism did not suddenly appear full-blown overnight. At first it involved playing for staked wagers or money prizes, and as a way to supplement income from other sources. With the development of mass spectator sport, however, the commercialization of games became hard to resist. In our own time, the incredible premium placed on athletic skill in the professional sport environment has considerably altered the balance of power between owners and athletes. Players at the top of their game command astonishing salaries, and owners continue to profit handsomely from their investments, while those on the sidelines wonder what all this means for sport itself.

For working people, the development of professional sport in the industrial era was connected to the prevailing discourse about manly labour, the importance of maintaining artisanal production skills, and the right to a living wage. In the last quarter of the nineteenth century, workers on all fronts were confronting and resisting employers intent on reducing skilled to sweated labour. What capitalists understood as the specialization and simplification of production through mechanization and 'scientific' management, workers understood as deskilling and an assault on their liberty. Yet in the sporting workplace, specialization meant not deskilling, but rather its opposite. No wonder, therefore, that workers were attracted to the sporting diamond: it was a place where they could demonstrate their physical skill and mental agility. For them, sport provided, literally, a level playing field, in the form of codified rules and the principles of fair play.

The highly nuanced discourse surrounding the term 'skill' helps explain why athletes who sold their athletic talents were regarded as 'professionals' rather than as 'workers.' There is little doubt that the term 'professional,' when applied to athletes, was meant to designate the opposite of 'amateur,' and to imply corruption and disreputability. Yet elsewhere in society the term 'professional' suggested authority, scientific knowledge, specialized training, independence, and self-regulation. There were many reasons, however, why the sporting professional was rarely able to claim the status of his counterpart in medicine, education, or the law. For one thing, professionalism in athletics was very much a function of the market; for another, it was rooted in the abilities of the body rather than those of the mind. Other professions attached themselves to notions of public service or claimed selfless dedication to science, the law, or even God; professional sportsmen, on the other hand, were perceived as motivated only by the dollar. At the same time, the specialized skills that athletes cultivated required a well-developed and physically coordinated body, and were much more transitory than the skills relating to the control of specialized knowledge. The skills of athletes always depended on the avoidance of injury, and quickly declined with the passing of time. Athletic skill was as much a function of age and sharp reflexes as it was of experience or strength, and players knew their professional careers could end quickly. Also, the erosion of skills was easy to measure; in the hands of employers, the statistical measurement of performance was a powerful instrument of control.

Of course, the vast majority of workers never aspired to careers as professional athletes. Most associated with the world of sport as consumers who paid money to watch sporting events, or they engaged in recreational sport. Some workers were not willing to accommodate themselves to the capitalist sport system, and sought out the alternatives offered by labour unions such as the International Workers of the World (the IWW or 'Wobblies') and the One Big Union (OBU). Both offered sporting programs to encourage worker solidarity and to provide greater access to recreation for working people. The most comprehensive Canadian sporting program of all was the one offered by the Worker's Sport Association (WSA), a frankly class-conscious worker's sport organization that grew out of the Communist International and was associated with the Communist Party of Canada (CPC) and Young Communist League (YCL). According to Bruce Kidd, the WSA represented opposition to – but not necessarily an alternative to – the bourgeois control of sport. By 1933 the association had 5,000 members across the country from New Waterford, Nova Scotia, to Ladysmith, British Columbia, and was offering a range of sports from soccer and softball to gymnastics, wrestling, and boxing. The WSA's visibility reached its peak during Hitler's Berlin Olympics of 1936. The WSA criticized that event not only because it was manipulating sport to promote fascist ends, but also because of the emphasis on high-performance athletics that characterized the Olympic movement in general. Eventually the WSA fell victim to the war and to the red-baiting that accompanied the Cold War. According to Kidd, however, the movement provided an important critique of the capitalist organization of sport and 'warmly welcomed and affirmed workers and their interests. Member clubs provided much needed recreational opportunities for a sizeable number of people who did not enjoy access to, could not afford, and were not very welcome in the middle-class, pro-British institutions that dominated amateur sports.'

Early Capitalist Sport

Workers were often uneasy about the capitalist control of sport, yet they were never able to mount a significant challenge to capitalist hegemony: ownership and control over the sporting marketplace remained firmly in capitalist hands. As businessmen came to control the important venues where games could be held, charging admission, paying athletes, and selling leisure to consumers as entertainment, sport became a business much like any other. Obviously there was money to be made in sport and in the associated industries that profited from sport's expansion. Yet no comprehensive study has yet been made of sport's economic impact in Canada between Confederation and the First World War. We know too little about how much profit sports promoters made from the various sporting activities from prizefighting to hockey games, and about how much compensation professional athletes were able to command. We know much more about the ideological motives of sport promoters, and about how workers, women, and ethnic minorities were represented in discourses about sport, than we do about the materialist underpinnings of the expanding sporting culture.

Recently, Tony Joyce has attempted to remedy this deficiency in his investigation of 'sport and the cash nexus' in nineteenth-century Toronto. He observes that the connections between sport and the market were evident as early as the building of Toronto's first taverns. The animal baits, prize fights, and post-game celebrations that often took place in them increased the publican's revenues and offered a chance for profit to promoters and athletes as well. In the 1850s and 1860s, private bath and swimming houses, ice rinks, racetracks, and other venues attached sport and recreation to the goal of capital accumulation. Yet at the time, many capitalists were uneasy about the popularization of sport, fearing that it would lead to higher absentee rates and a demand for a shorter working day. Once entrepreneurs realized there was money to be made from the public's seemingly insatiable demand for sporting entertainment, this uneasiness gradually subsided. Joyce notes there was a rapid trend toward the commercialization of sport in the two decades after Confederation: 'By the late 1800s, Toronto's sporting zeitgeist was indistinguishable from the cut-throat, day to day activities of brokers, commission merchants, lawyers, petty merchants, and big-time entrepreneurs.'

The expanding sporting universe of the late nineteenth century had economic spinoffs for various businesses. There was money to be made from manufacturing sports equipment: ice and roller skates, uniforms and swimsuits, boots and shoes, bats, balls, lacrosse and hockey sticks, billiard tables, bicycles, fishing and mountain climbing gear, guns for hunting, boats, sleighs, toboggans, harness-racing sulkies, bowling pins, helmets, protective padding, and the ubiquitous jockstrap. Although the giant American sporting goods companies offered a wide variety of equipment to Canadians, there were a number of successful Canadian enterprises that served the sporting market. Under Macdonald's national policy, established in 1879, Canadian legislators moved to protect industries of this sort through tariffs. Also, sporting contests had immediate economic spin-offs in the communities where they were held. Many businesses and occupations profited from Toronto's burgeoning sporting environment; Joyce specifically cites photographers, printers, reporters, policemen, gamblers, pool sellers, telegraphers, blacksmiths, harness makers, stewards, carpenters, labourers, caretakers, illuminators, railways, steamers, newspapers, taverns, hotels, manufacturers of uniforms, shoes, and equipment, ticket sellers, lawyers, doctors, architects, salesmen, veterinarians, grooms, managers, and refreshment sellers, and the athletes themselves.

Gamblers

Many of these subsidiary occupations and businesses were a natural outgrowth of the expanding business order; in contrast, gamblers, speculators, and professional athletes were a direct creation of sport – and were often excoriated for their unsavoury behaviour. Indeed, one could argue that the moral discourse around gambling and crooked speculation helped legitimize the expansion of sport as a business enterprise. To an entrepreneurial middle class committed to the ethic of hard work, religious duty, thrift, and self-improvement, gambling seemed both irrational and corrupt. In Britain, the middle-class attack on gambling was directed upwards toward the dissolute aristocracy, who, it was suggested, preferred idle amusement to hard work, as well as downwards toward the working class, among whom gambling constituted a threat to the family economy. Petty betting was especially popular among working men; for them, it was a way to declare loyalty to the home team, as well as a chance to make a little extra pocket money. Ross McKibbin has described popular betting on sporting events as an example of a working-class tradition of self-help. In Canada, neither middle-class reformers nor politicians saw gambling in this light: they attacked it, with the goal of stabilizing workers' incomes and keeping sport free of corruption.

Gambling at sporting events was widespread in Canada, and may sometimes have been more attractive to patrons than the sport itself. Dog and horsetracks, unauthorized prizefights and animal baits, and baseball, lacrosse, and hockey games all attracted the gambling fraternity. In his study of Vulcan, Alberta, Paul Voisey associates gambling with the speculative nature of frontier life, and notes that baseball games were surrounded by heavy betting, sometimes involving wagers of hundreds of dollars and even quarter sections of farmland. Yet it is questionable whether the West was much different from the East in this regard: anywhere there was sport in Canada, there were gamblers. Newspaper reports routinely deplored the extent of betting that surrounded these events. Yet by drawing attention to the practice – and in lurid detail at that – they may unwittingly have been fostering it. Reporters often estimated the amount of money that changed hands, reported rumours of big winnings, and even commented on the odds being offered. Descriptions of thrown matches, of players 'not trying,' and of referee favouritism were also common.

Athletes were by no means immune from the lure of quick money, and when the odds were favourable they

sometimes arranged for friends to place bets against them.
Sometimes players actually colluded with crooked gamblers. For example, in 1890 a well-known gambler from
Halifax named Frank Robinson and an unnamed Saint
John man fixed the Maritime baseball championship. However, baseball was no more infected by the gambling spirit
than lacrosse, hockey, rowing, and cycling. Before the First
World War, gambling was associated with *any* popular sporting event, especially if the teams or individual competitors
were of relatively equal ability or the match drew large
crowds. And because so much betting was informal and
subterranean, it was hard to combat.

The difficulty in regulating gambling was especially evident in horseracing. Gambling had been associated with
horseracing since colonial times, often involving wagers
between horse owners and side bets by interested onlook-
ers. With the development of modern commercialized racetracks came a movement to formalize racetrack betting
and make it the exclusive preserve of the racing associations or jockey clubs that ran the tracks. Gambling may
have been a blight on the working class, but among the
elite who patronized racetracks it apparently could be tolerated. In the years before the First World War there were
occasional crusades to outlaw betting at racetracks, but the
movement in Canada was far less effective than the one in
the United States, where many tracks were forced to close,
having been deprived of gambling revenues. In Canada,
the most significant challenge to gamblers came in 1909–
10, when a gambling bill sponsored by the Moral and Social Reform Council of Canada was introduced in Parlia-
ment to criminalize bookmaking at Canadian racetracks.
After considerable debate, the bill was amended to allow betting at tracks, but not off-track betting. What had
been at stake here was the incredible profits being made
by the major thoroughbred racecourses. What was achieved
was the state-sanctioned institutionalization of racetrack
gambling. In later years, the introduction of pari-mutuel
betting machines and the legalization of off-track bet-

ting would strengthen the links between gambling and the racetrack.

During the interwar years, gambling and horseracing continued to be closely associated. Right through the Depression, large crowds attended tracks across the country. Betting revenues increased both in thoroughbred racing and at standardbred tracks. According to Suzanne Morton, the First World War and the Depression had weakened people's belief in a comprehensible and predictable world; having lost their faith in the economic system, people grew more willing to depend on luck as a way of making their way through life. Lotteries, bingo, raffles, sweepstakes, and racetrack gambling had a high profile in Canada during the Depression. The Irish Sweepstakes, organized initially as a way to raise money for Irish sailors lost at sea, was reorganized in 1930 as an international lottery in which ticket numbers were matched with horses in British races and prizewinning derived from how they placed. The success of these sweepstakes led to growing support for state lotteries in Canada as a way to stem the drain of capital out of the country; however, the antigambling lobby was strong enough to defeat any such initiatives. Yet despite the opposition of the courts, the churches, and most politicians, gambling continued unabated. 'The persistence and popularity of lotteries, sweepstakes, raffles and bingo,' Morton suggests 'verify the continuation of an oppositional culture, for their continuance can also be regarded as a simultaneous form of cultural resistance and a response to vulnerability.'

The gambling subculture was flourishing just as the more popular team sports were distancing themselves from gamblers. Baseball's famous Black Sox scandal, which centred on the throwing of the 1919 World Series, provided baseball's new commissioner, Judge Kenesaw Mountain Landis, with the opportunity to establish baseball's public respectability and protect its integrity. The owners of professional baseball and hockey franchises did not depend on gambling revenues for their profits, and found it in their interest to attack gambling's nefarious influence. Having cleansed their own Augean stables of gambling corruption, the owners found it easier to defend themselves against charges of robber-baron capitalism and to present themselves as high-minded captains of the sporting industry. For the owners of NHL clubs – some of whom, like Jimmy Norris, had close associations with the 'mob' – it was important to look like respectable businessmen, as it helped them ruthlessly assert control over the community-based clubs and rival leagues that existed between the wars.

Amateurs and Professionals

The debate about gambling and sport was also linked to the continuing debate in Canada over amateurism and professionalism. According to the traditions of gentlemanly amateurism, sport was to be played for the love of the game and in keeping with the standards of gentlemanly behaviour. There was thus a strong aversion to cheaters, ringers, and those who placed winning, personal achievement, and financial gain above fair play. In the early years of organized sport, the amateur ideal carried exclusions based not only on playing for pay but also on class and ethnic identity. For example, in 1873 the Montreal Pedestrian Club defined an amateur athlete as one who had 'never competed in any open competition or for public money, or for admission money, or with professionals for a prize, public money or admission money, nor has ever, at any period of his life taught or assisted in the pursuit of Athletic exercises as a means of livelihood or is a laborer or an Indian.'

At the beginning of the twentieth century the major arbiter of the amateur principle in Canada was the Canadian Amateur Athletic Union (CAAU), established in 1898 to succeed the Amateur Athletic Association, which had operated since 1884. At that time, most of the major team sports were flirting with professionalism. Individual sports such as cycling and speed skating provided opportunities for both amateur and professional competitors, but kept them separate; professionalism in rowing was undisguised; and competitors in Caledonian competitions had for decades been competing for prize money. Established to protect amateur athletics from the further incursion of professionalism, the CAAU initially claimed jurisdiction over seventeen sports. It investigated violations of the amateur code, suspended violators, and reinstated those who agreed to put professionalism behind them and to accept the amateur definition in its entirety. In the first decade of the century the CAAU became embroiled in a dispute with the Montreal Amateur Athletic Association (MAAA) over the provision in the amateur code that prohibited amateurs from competing with or against professionals. Breaking away from the CAAU, the Montrealers created the Amateur Athletic Federation of Canada (AAFC), and for two years between 1906 and 1908 the two groups fought an 'athletic war' over the meaning of amateurism. The CAAU, which adhered to the amateur code in its entirety and thus refused to allow competition between amateurs and professionals, eventually triumphed over the AAFC and absorbed it into the new AAU of Canada in 1909.

Bruce Kidd's fine study of the development of national sporting organizations in Canada, *The Struggle for Canadian Sport*, contends that the AAU was an important nation-building institution that despite its middle-class biases served as a brake on the development of a full-market system of capitalist sport in Canada. 'Up until the early 1930s amateurism was a system that worked, at least for the class that championed it,' Kidd argues. Among other things, 'it placed an effective limit on the amount of time and energy the top athletes had to devote to training, enabling them to prepare simultaneously for a post-sport profession.' But the Depression seriously weakened the forces of amateurism. During the economic crisis, athletes often found it hard to resist under-the-table-payments or reimbursement for time away from work (broken-time payments). Equally attractive were the jobs that were sometimes offered in return for playing for a company team. What is clear in this is that amateurism itself carried a price tag. For those who had athletic skills with market value, but who worked and struggled just to make a living, the price of maintaining one's amateur status was often too high.

Sport and Consumerism

Attempts to maintain the principles of amateurism between the wars ran counter to the advancing tide of commercialism in North America. Indeed, the interwar years witnessed the consolidation of sport as the most commanding element in the modern, commercialized mass leisure marketplace. Of course, the foundations for the explosion of sport after the First World War had been laid much earlier. Before the war, the expansion of urban transportation networks – especially electric tram service – allowed more and more people to attend sporting events. Railways offered excursion fares that enabled fans to follow their teams from town to town; this heightened urban rivalries and stimulated community boosterism. Special train services were provided to get people to important matches. In her study of Vancouver's interurban railway, Barbara Schrodt describes how BC Electric converted open flat-bed cars into 'lacrosse trains' that carried spectators to New Westminster for 25¢. Promoters were thus able to lure 15,000 or more fans to the Queen's Park exhibition grounds. The Canadian Pacific Railway went so far as to hire sports agent Joe Page, instructing him to encourage leagues and teams across the country to associate themselves formally with the National Association of Professional Baseball leagues in the United States (referred to colloquially as 'organized baseball'). For railway companies like the CPR, which were always looking for ways to increase traffic, financially secure leagues in baseball, hockey, and lacrosse were obviously a good thing.

The 1920s witnessed the rise of consumer culture. New technologies such as radio and motion pictures manufactured hopes of new prosperity. Assembly line technologies turned out a vast new array of consumer goods, from home appliances to automobiles; and the all-pervasive advertising industry employed new techniques to encourage a culture of consumption. Newspapers hired employees to sell ad space; thus, the promotion of new products became an increasingly important characteristic of the modern press. Newspapers also expanded their sports sections, which indirectly advertised games as commodities for consumption; the heightened interest that resulted from this coverage swelled audiences at sporting events. According to Mark Dyreson, sport in the postwar era was no longer understood to be a social technology that would help create progressive communities; rather, it was considered a form of entertainment that contributed to individual self-fulfilment and happiness and allowed escape from the drudgeries of life. In the twenties, Dyreson writes, 'athletics were described as an end and not a means. In consumer culture sport had come to be viewed as one of modern life's central purposes.' As Victorian notions of social responsibility gave way to the hedonism of the roaring twenties, sport was gradually detached from the mission of social rehabilitation.

Professional Baseball

The reimagining of sport as an entertainment device rather than an instrument for reform signalled its closer attachment to the market and its increasing submission to the demands of capital. Professional baseball and hockey flourished after the First World War across the country. This was by no means a sudden phenomenon. Professional baseball in Canada dates back to the 1870s, when promoters like brewer George Sleeman of the Guelph Maple Leafs and oilman Jacob Englehart of the London Tecumsehs invested in high-calibre players, paid for equipment, lined up games against quality opponents from other cities, and paid their teams' travel expenses. Baseball clubs in Winnipeg, Saint John, and Halifax were all importing American professionals by 1878 – a practice followed in the next decade by teams across Canada, from Moncton and Fredericton in the east to Victoria and Kamloops in the west. By the 1880s full-fledged professional clubs were operating in Toronto, Montreal, and Vancouver, and there were semiprofessional leagues on the prairies, in Quebec, and in the Maritimes. These leagues offered itinerant professionals and American college students a chance to make money during the summer months, and often were on a par with or even better than some organized leagues. In 1890, for example, the Saint John Shamrocks' eleven-man roster was made up exclusively of American imported players, five of whom would go on to play big-league baseball in the National League.

By the time the First World War broke out, baseball in most of Canada's larger cities had succumbed to the lure of gate money and profit. In his study of the 1908 Vancouver Beavers of the professional North West League, Robin Anderson suggests that 'league organization, scheduling, player personnel, team performance, and the character and motives of many spectators were shaped by the drive to make money.' At the time, most civic leaders believed that a successful professional franchise was good advertising for the community. For instance, in its report on the professional Western Canada Baseball League (with teams in Winnipeg, Edmonton, Calgary, Brandon, Saskatoon, and Moose Jaw, and the prospect of a revived franchise in Lethbridge), the 1912 *Spalding Guide* linked a competitive professional ball club with future civic progress.

In Lethbridge, for example, a growing population, a fine new streetcar service, and the potential for future growth demanded a good ball team, even if it meant an initial investment that would not immediately be recovered. 'What is a few hundred dollars loss at this particular time,' the *Guide* asked, 'when shortly it means not only a great financial success, but, in addition, an advertising medium ... that is of untold value to ... [Lethbridge] and its business interests?' Clearly, the new discourse about baseball's social purpose focused more on the community's future economic development than on character building, respectability, and moral improvement – concerns that had preoccupied so many commentators before the turn of the last century.

In the interwar years, a number of Canadian cities and towns had franchises in baseball's professional minor leagues. The Toronto Maple Leafs baseball club, which had played in the professional Eastern league from about the turn of the century, and then in the International League beginning in 1912, was the most successful baseball franchise in the country between the wars and would continue to operate into the 1960s. Montreal had teams in a number of different pro leagues between the turn of the century and the Second World War; the most successful of these was founded in 1928, when a group of investors led by Althanase David and Ernest Savard purchased the Syracuse club of the International League and moved it to Montreal as the Royals. In 1931 an ownership group that included Montreal businessmen Hector Racine, Romeo Gauvreau, and Charles Trudeau (the father of Prime Minister Pierre Elliott Trudeau) bought the club, operating it until 1938, when they sold it to the Brooklyn Dodgers, who would run it as their premier farm club. Besides the teams in Toronto and Montreal, there were interwar professional franchises in Vancouver, Edmonton, Calgary, Winnipeg, Brandon, Kitchener, Hamilton, London, Ottawa, Quebec City, Trois-Rivières, Sydney, New Waterford, Glace Bay, and Dominion.

The great popularity of professional baseball between the wars spilled over into baseball at all levels. Commercial and industrial leagues, youth teams, semiprofessional community baseball teams, and itinerant barnstorming clubs flourished across the United States and Canada. The 1921 edition of Spalding's *Canadian Baseball Guide* reported that the independent Montreal City Baseball League was 'one of the strongest organizations in semi-professional Base Ball,' drawing more than 75,000 paid admissions the previous season. In Toronto the same year, the Toronto Playgrounds Base Ball Leagues had a total of 135 teams, and the number increased each year thereafter. In Manitoba, local senior league games averaged over 2,500 attendance. Farther east in the Maritimes, almost every small town fielded a team for the Maritime amateur championship, while rising to the challenge provided by touring clubs from New England. At the time, Maritime baseball was well enough respected that the major league Boston Braves travelled north in the middle of their major league schedule to play the Maritime champion St Stephen club in 1934, and the Yarmouth Gateways the following year. The baseball connection between the Maritimes and New England is instructive, but not necessarily unique. While baseball reached into all corners of the country, it was also relatively regional in character and lacked a national organizational framework. Rather than establishing links across the country from east to west, baseball – even in its amateur or semiprofessional form – drew Canadians into the orbit of the increasingly commercialized sporting world.

Barnstormers

The interwar period was the heyday of baseball barnstorming, especially by teams of Black players, many of whom also played in the Negro Leagues in the United States, and occasionally took to the road to supplement their income and demonstrate their skills. As Donn Rogosin has observed, 'the majority of games played by Negro league teams were not ... league games but instead exhibitions held wherever a profitable afternoon beckoned. It was pure economics: white people had more money.' During the 1920s and 1930s, many of these clubs crossed into Canada to play for a guaranteed purse or a portion of the gate. Thus Canadians had a chance to appreciate the skills of great African-American players like Satchel Paige, Josh Gibson, and 'Cool Papa' Bell. 'Chappie' Johnson's Colored All-Stars, the Philadelphia Colored Giants, the New York Black Yankees, the Boston Royal Giants, the Cuban Giants, the Ethiopian Clowns, and the Zulu Cannibal Giants thrilled audiences with their smooth style of play, and with trick plays such as bunting with the end of the bat. Yet clowning and buffoonery could also reinforce racial stereotypes and notions of Black inferiority. Caught as they were in the contradictions of a white marketplace, Black players often found it necessary to create an image of 'otherness' in order to attract fans.

Many of these barnstormers toured with or played against the bizarre House of David teams, which criss-crossed Canada and the United States every season. Playing on ethnic and sectarian imagery as a way to dramatize their difference and attract larger gates, the House of David players sported bushy whiskers that hung to belt level. The players served as advertising for the religious teachings of Benjamin Purnell, the self-proclaimed sixth son of the House of David, who ran a religious colony in Benton Harbour, Michigan, whose members, among other things, abstained from sexual intercourse. When it came to baseball, Purnell – whose charlatanism was later exposed when he was convicted of rape and sentenced to prison – had few scruples about hiring ringers to play for him. Among those who played for House of David teams were Grover Cleveland Alexander, Elmer Dean (brother of major leaguer 'Dizzy' Dean), Larry Jansen, and even 'Babe' Didrikson Zaharias, America's greatest female athlete of the day.

The touring Black baseball teams from south of the border gave Canadians a chance to admire the skills of players
who were barred by their colour from playing in professional baseball. Meanwhile, a number of Canadian-born
Black players were demonstrating their abilities on the diamond. One of the most talented of these was Vincent
'Manny' McIntyre of Fredericton, whose career began with
a New Brunswick junior club in 1938. Equally at home on
the baseball field and the hockey rink, McIntyre went on to
play both baseball and hockey as a professional. After the
war, he played hockey on an all-Black line for the Sherbrooke
Aces, a Montreal farm club, along with the Carnegie brothers, Herb and Ossie. Despite the talent he and his linemates
possessed, none of them was ever invited to the Canadiens'
training camp. The colour bar in hockey was not broken
until 1958, when Willie O'Ree, another New Brunswick
native who starred locally in hockey and baseball, started
for the NHL's Boston Bruins.

In 1946 McIntyre found himself caught up in what Jules
Tygiel has described as 'baseball's great experiment,' when
general manager Branch Rickey of the Brooklyn Dodgers
signed Jackie Robinson and four other African-American
ballplayers to professional contracts. Robinson began his
professional career in Montreal, where – so the Dodgers
believed – he would receive more respectful treatment and
less abuse than in American cities. After leading the Royals
to the International League pennant, he became the first
Black ballplayer of the modern era to play in the majors.
'Jackie has been one of the greatest ambassadors of good-
will,' wrote Cal Best in the *Clarion*, an important Black
voice in the fight against racial discrimination in Canada.
'He has proven himself with all the decorum and dignity
that is necessary in the face of the greatest obstacles.'

Often overlooked in all the testimonies to Robinson is
the contribution that Manny McIntyre and Fred Thomas
made to breaking the colour bar in baseball's minor
leagues. In 1946 McIntyre was signed by the Cincinnati

Reds organization, making him one of only six players of colour in all of organized baseball. McIntyre joined a Reds farm team and broke the colour bar in the Border League, playing for Sherbrooke. Feeling shunned by his American team-mates, he quit the team, and signed with the Cuban Giants of the American Negro Baseball League as a replacement for Minnie Minoso, who had gone on to the majors. Thomas, a native of Windsor, Ontario, signed with the Cleveland Indians and broke the colour bar in the Eastern League. Fred Thomas was a multisport athlete. As a six-foot-two centre on Assumption College's basketball team, he broke the 2,000 point mark in his college career. He was invited to play for the Harlem Globetrotters and did so briefly. He was also courted by the Montreal Alouettes and Toronto Argonauts of the Canadian Football League.

In the decade after the Second World War, professional baseball flourished across Canada, just as it did in the United States. The Montreal and Toronto franchises in the International League had continued to operate throughout the war, despite the significant scaling back of professional baseball. In peacetime they were rejoined by Canadian teams in a number of baseball leagues, including the Northern League, the Western International League, the Border League, the Canadian American League, and various 'outlaw leagues,' which relied on a mix of old pros and college players (examples: the Quebec Provincial League and the Halifax and District League). By 1960, minor league baseball had contracted significantly as television pulled fans into the privacy of their homes. After that, professional baseball would be largely confined to the bigger markets across the country such as Vancouver, Edmonton, Calgary, Winnipeg, Montreal, and Toronto. When major league baseball began expanding into new markets, Canada was granted its first major league franchise: the Montreal Expos joined baseball's National League for the 1969 season. Then in 1977 the Toronto Blue Jays entered the American League.

The National Hockey League

Like baseball, hockey in Canada was beset by professionalism in the interwar years. At the turn of the last century,
hockey was still experiencing the tension between amateur
and professional influences that characterized other sports,
from rowing and cycling to baseball and lacrosse. By 1910
the game was increasingly being tailored to suit the objectives of capitalist promoters. A number of professional
hockey leagues emerged between 1900 and the end of the
First World War, and while only a few lasted long, they
suggested that hockey would eventually become part of
the developing capitalist sport nexus. The earliest official
professional league was the International Hockey League
(IHL), established in 1904 with teams in Pittsburgh,
Houghton, Calumet, and Sault St Marie. It was followed by
the Eastern Canadian Hockey League (1906) and by professional leagues in Ontario and the Maritimes. Daniel Mason contends that while the early IHL operated for only
three seasons, it nonetheless provided 'a model of how a
professional league could be operated ... [and] forced elite
amateur hockey associations in Canada to weigh the mer-
its of upholding amateurism or paying players to maintain
a competitive team.' On the west coast, a lumber baron
named Joe Patrick established the Pacific Coast League in
1912; with his sons Lester and Frank, he operated it as
'syndicate hockey.' The Patrick family ran the league under a unified management, shifting teams from location to
location as they saw fit and sending the players they signed
to wherever they were needed most.

The most significant league to emerge was of course the
National Hockey League, which rose in 1917 from the
ashes of the eight-year-old National Hockey Association.
According to Bruce Kidd, from its inception the league
placed economics ahead of the interests of both hockey
and the community. It followed a deliberate strategy of
destroying its competitors or at least driving them into
subservience. A full-market capitalist organization, the NHL

had to expand its audience to pay for players, venues, equipment, and team travel. To protect their profit margins, the owners built new arenas with enlarged seating capacity, installed artificial ice plants that permitted a longer season, scheduled games for the most advantageous times, and raised ticket prices as necessary. New arenas included the Montreal Forum (1924), Madison Square Garden (1925), the Detroit Olympia (1928), and Maple Leaf Gardens (1931), which had almost twice the seating capacity of Toronto's old Mutual Street Arena. The lure of profit also meant expansion to the United States, where American sports moguls were ready to purchase franchises. Charles Adams bought the Boston franchise in 1924 for $15,000. Then in 1925, well-known boxing promoter Tex Rickard purchased the Hamilton franchise, including its players, for $75,000 and transferred it to New York. The new Chicago Black Hawks and Detroit Red Wings franchises eventually fell under the control of Arthur Wirtz and James Norris respectively. Like Rickard, these men were prominent boxing promoters. Faced with this kind of competition and financial might, the owners of the small-market clubs in Ottawa, Quebec City, and Hamilton read the writing on the wall and sold off their players to the new franchises – at a profit. (Ottawa, one of the founding members of the NHL, held out until 1934; that year, facing financial difficulties, owner Frank Ahearne sold the club to a St Louis syndicate.)

In the interwar period the NHL was the dominant league in North America, but its influence was confined to the eastern half of the continent. The NHL's main rivals were the Patricks' Pacific Coast League; which had franchises in coastal cities on both sides of the border; the Western Canada Hockey League (1922), with teams in Calgary, Edmonton, Regina, and Saskatoon; and the American Hockey League, founded in 1927. In 1925 the Pacific Coast League collapsed, and its Victoria and Vancouver teams joined the WHL. The WHL dissolved the following year, and sold its best players to the NHL at a significant profit. Under a new management team headed by Frank Calder, the NHL then proceeded to assert itself as the premier professional league in North America. By the early 1930s the league was refusing to accept challenges for the Stanley Cup; thus, supremacy in hockey in North America was identified with the NHL alone. At the same time, it moved to turn other leagues such as the rival AHL into minor leagues. The tacit agreement was that the NHL would not compete in the markets of rival leagues, but in return the NHL would be given the right to draft one player from each minor league club for $5,000 every other year.

Throughout the Depression, there was some franchise instability, but by the end of the Second World War, the NHL had consolidated its operations in six locations, often referred to today as 'the original six.' Given that the NHL had confined itself to six major markets, and to only Montreal and Toronto in Canada, it should not be surprising that amateur, senior, and community-based hockey remained a vital component in Canadian hockey. The Canadian Amateur Hockey Association (CAHA) was the governing body for amateur hockey. During the 1920s it continued to adhere to traditional notions of amateurism. However, as hockey's popularity grew over the next decade, the CAHA abandoned its allegiance to strict amateurism: it accepted the idea of 'broken time' payments, which compensated players for time lost at work, and allowed players in senior hockey to be paid. This compromise allowed the CAHA to survive as a competitor to the NHL and to maintain its jurisdiction over junior and senior hockey and international competitions. After the Second World War, community-based hockey continued to flourish, and the Allan Cup – Canada's championship trophy for senior hockey – retained its prestige. But by the 1960s, the CAHA's authority was being brought into question as Canadian teams faced tough competition on the international scene from the Czechs, Swedes, and Russians. At the same time, NHL expansion was diluting the talent base for senior hockey.

The NHL kept its reputation as a major league during these years, even though it remained a six-team league confined to the northeastern part of the continent. In the United States, major league baseball and the National Football League became committed to franchise expansion, lured by the prospect of lucrative television contracts and as a response to the threat of rival leagues; the NHL was obliged to follow suit. In 1967 the NHL doubled its number of teams to twelve by adding six new American teams. Over the next seven years, it added another six teams. This attracted interest from American television networks, although hockey's limited popularity in the south has continued to affect contract negotiations between the league and the major networks. In Canada, television was a strength rather than a problem, as the major networks competed for the right to carry hockey broadcasts.

By 1974 the NHL had grown to eighteen teams, yet only Vancouver had been added to the league's Canadian contingent. The NHL's failure to cultivate the Canadian market, coupled with growing prosperity in western Canada, provided an opening for promoters Bill Hunter and Ben Hatskin to threaten the authority of the NHL by establishing a rival league. In 1972 they launched the World Hockey Association (WHA) with franchises in every corner of the continent, from Miami to Oakland and from New York to Los Angeles. More significantly, there were Canadian franchises in Toronto, Edmonton, Calgary, and Winnipeg. At first, the WHA seemed unlikely to succeed, but this changed dramatically when Hatskin's Winnipeg Jets signed Bobby Hull, 'The Golden Jet,' to a multimillion-dollar contract. The WHA competed for pre-eminence with the NHL until it collapsed in 1979. Many of its Canadian franchises were absorbed into the NHL.

During the 1970s the NHL also established a presence on the international hockey scene. By the 1960s it had become painfully obvious that Canada could not compete successfully in world championship competition without sending its best players. In 1962 the CAHA had adopted a plan for a national hockey team made up of senior, junior, and university players. The experiment was the brainchild of Father David Bauer, who was determined to establish a team motivated by national allegiance and committed to good sportsmanship. It was a noble idea, but it did not bring the desired results, largely because the NHL was unwilling to cooperate with the national program. Fed up with its inability to compete effectively, the CAHA finally chose to disband the national team and withdraw from world championship competition. When the Soviet Union agreed to an eight-game series against Canada's best professional players, the NHL eagerly plunged into international competition. For most Canadian hockey fans the 1972 series was a defining moment. When Paul Henderson scored the winning goal with thirty-four seconds left in the final game, thus propelling Canada to victory, the result was an outpouring of national feeling that reminded us what hockey meant to us as Canadians. It was also a defining moment for hockey: from that time on, professional hockey was on the ascendancy, not just at home but around the world.

Except for Toronto, Vancouver, and Montreal, NHL franchises in Canada have had their difficulties over the past decade. Quebec City and Winnipeg have lost their teams, and owners in Ottawa and Edmonton have threatened to sell to American investors if they do not receive public support. The difficulties facing the Canadian clubs are connected to the larger processes of capitalist consolidation and to prevailing market forces on the North American continent. In recent years the NHL has been following a new, marketing oriented 'Sunbelt strategy,' designed to bring the game into new markets in the American south. The sale of the Winnipeg Jets and the team's transfer to Phoenix is an example of this strategy. Jim Silver, leader of the Thin Ice coalition in Winnipeg, which criticized the

Save the Jets campaign for its willingness to bow to the whims of corporations, observed that 'the same powerful market forces that marginalized the Jets in a rapidly changing NHL are marginalizing Winnipeg in an increasingly continentalized economy.'

Canadian Football

In hockey, the transition to the professional game was well underway by the 1920s. In football, on the other hand, tension continued between amateur ideals, allegiance to the community and nation, and playing for pay. Football players began turning pro in significant numbers in the 1930s. Before that time, the game still resembled rugby more than modern football, and, with its long tradition in Canadian colleges and universities, it still had strong roots in amateur sport. University teams dominated Canadian football well into the 1920s. As the game developed, two groups debated its future. On the one side stood the traditionalists, who wanted to maintain rugby's English character; on the other stood the liberals, who hoped to incorporate some features of the American game into Canadian rugby football. Most of the liberals were in the West, which had a weaker tradition of university football and as well as weaker ties to Britain. In Ontario, feelings were mixed, but generally there was considerable resistance to embracing the American game in its entirety. In the Maritimes, rugby remained in the ascendancy.

The Canadian game was influenced by coaches imported from the United States, such as Frank Shaughnessy, who coached McGill from 1912 to 1919. Shaughnessy introduced the football huddle to the Canadian game in 1925 and was an advocate of the forward pass. In 1929 the Canadian Rugby Union rules committee decided to give a modified forward pass a trial, and at the same time to increase the size of the ball to make it conform to the American game. Two years later the forward pass was accepted in its entirety, and the term 'touchdown' was introduced to replace the rugby term 'try.' Warren Stevens and Lew Hayman made their way north from the United States to coach Canadians in forward passing and blocking techniques, and a number of teams recruited American players.

The debate between traditionalists and liberals continued. The influence of the traditionalists was strong enough to arrest the drift toward the complete Americanization of the Canadian game. In 1936 the CRU limited the number of imports to five per team, and ruled that only players who had lived in Canada for at least a year would be eligible for Grey Cup play. The constraints that were placed on outright professionalism and Americanization in the interwar years have had a lasting impact on the Canadian game. Canadian football after the Second World War was characterized by import quotas, a mixture of payments to players and off-field employment opportunities, and a rules code that differed from the American one. In the 1950s, standardized Canadian rules were adopted that were acceptable to both east and west, and this paved the way for the establishment of the Canadian Football League in 1958, with Sydney Halter as league commissioner.

In recent years the CFL has struggled to define itself. On the one hand it is a professional league motivated by the desire for profit; on the other it has always attempted to serve community interests and Canadian identity. In the 1960s and 1970s it was possible to achieve both ends because of the widespread popularity of football throughout North America, but competition for the entertainment dollar over the past two decades has been fierce. Most CFL clubs today, both the privately owned franchises and the community-owned operations in Saskatchewan, Edmonton, and Winnipeg, are happy to break even from year to year. For that reason many investors are unwilling to stay in the game over the long haul.

The long-standing financial problems of the league have also made it vulnerable to fly-by-night speculators who try to make it more than it can be. In the mid-1980s, Vancouver real estate magnate Nelson Skalbania bought the Montreal Alouettes and embarked on a project to raise the profile of the CFL in the United States and land a lucrative television deal south of the border. But his highly publicized signings of American stars Vince Ferragamo, Billy 'White Shoes' Johnson, and David Overstreet failed to result in success either on the field or at the gate. Soon after, the Alouettes folded, after forty distinguished years of play. This scenario was repeated in 1991 when Bruce McNall, owner of the NHL's Los Angeles Kings, purchased the Toronto Argonauts and brought Raghib 'Rocket' Ismail to Toronto in a bid to revitalize football in the CFL's primary market. For this effort, McNall enlisted the support of partners Wayne Gretzky and comedian John Candy, and at first all went well: the Argos won the 1991 Grey Cup and attendance soared. But these successes could not be sustained. The Argos won only six games in 1992 and three in 1993. By then the city had soured on the team. McNall himself was in deep financial difficulty (he subsequently served prison time for his illegal business practices). Canadian football in Toronto is now at its lowest level of popularity since the CFL began operating forty years ago.

In the 1990s, the CFL continued to face economic hardships, and tensions continued to grow between the profit motive and the league's traditional allegiance to community and nation. In a desperate attempt to reverse its economic fortunes, the CFL expanded into the United States, admitting Sacramento to the league in 1993 and Las Vegas, Baltimore, Birmingham, Memphis, San Antonio, and Shreveport over the next two years. The league barely survived the debacle that followed, and even had the experiment succeeded the result would likely have been the end of Canada's distinctive brand of football. The league has since reduced its expectations and has rededicated itself to those traditions that have long sustained it. What it offers is a wide-open game that contrasts favourably to the plodding style of American football. It is not yet known whether a professional league with salary caps, import restrictions, and slim profits for investors can survive in the sporting marketplace of the twenty-first century. This question is connected to the larger issue of whether Canada itself can survive in the age of global capitalism.

Conclusion

Since the middle of the nineteenth century there has been a growing affinity between sport and the marketplace in Canada. Connected to this has been a debate over ownership: Who should own sport, and for what purpose? In this chapter I have tried to demonstrate that this debate has always existed. Before the First World War, sporting discourses centred on amateurism and professionalism, respectability and rowdyism, capitalist enterprise and working class fraternalism, manly character and civic worth, community identity and economic development. Sport had obvious economic benefits, and provided business opportunities for large and small capitalists alike; yet there were many who believed that when sport was attached to the market, its potential for encouraging social responsibility and moral improvement was undermined. For elite sportsmen, the amateur tradition constituted a defence against the win-at-all-costs professionalism and rowdy spectators, and ensured that sport would not be diffused downward to the working class. Workers, for their part, turned to sport as a means of demonstrating their own self-worth and respectability, and of combatting the more demeaning prejudices of those bourgeois improvers who wished to colonize the leisure pursuits of the working class in the interest of respectability and order.

After the First World War, sport was more closely linked to the emerging consumer society and to notions of personal happiness and fulfilment. Increasingly, corporations and individual capitalists were turning high-performance sport into a commodity and presenting it for sale in the marketplace. This process was encouraged by newspapers and radio and eventually by television. By venerating competitive sporting performance, the media helped fashion a cult of athletic heroes; it then made those heroes available to the reading, listening, and watching public. Today's sporting hero is likely to be a professional athlete who commands a colossal salary and endorsement revenues, but this was not always the case. Before the Second World War it was still possible to accommodate amateurism and high-performance athletics and at least partly resist attempts by capitalist promoters to control high-level sport for profit. Examples of the constraints against full-blown professionalism are numerous, but nowhere are they more evident than in the Olympic Games. Yet as recent events have demonstrated, the games themselves have succumbed to commercial interests. Over the past two decades the IOC has ended its restrictions against the involvement of professionals, having recognized the hypocrisy of maintaining amateurism for athletes when the games have become a commercialized circus.

To understand this transition, we must turn our attention away from those who promote, administer, and play sport, and consider those who consume it. In the next chapter I focus upon those who cheered sport on, idealized their athletic heroes, and in the process made sport a fundamental component of Canadian life and the contemporary social order.

4

Cheers

Sport in Canada would not be what it has become without spectators. Yet we still know little about the history of this aspect of sporting life. In our own time, spectatorism conjures up the sedentary lifestyle of the weekend couch potato, who sits glued to the television set with beer in hand and a belly exceeding the belt line. Understood in this way, spectatorism seems little more than a social narcotic, a celebration of the voyeuristic and inactive life. Some observers see spectator sport as a device applied by a manipulative ruling order to divert attention from the social price that its authority exerts. This jaundiced view of the spectator has a lengthy pedigree, and was a staple of the oldstyle Marxist critique of capitalist sport. It became popular again in the 1960s, when the 'counterculture' condemned sport as a handmaiden of militarism, physical violence, sexism, racism, and the capitalist establishment. The new left argued that sport was part of a process of cultural brainwashing that helped mould a docile citizenry unable to think critically about questions of social power. According to Paul Hoch, an American sociologist writing in the late 1960s, 'participation sports for the elite was gradually readapted into spectator consumption for ... "the masses" ... From the point of view of the ruling class, the sort of passive attitudes industrial workers learn in watching a baseball game serve as a useful socializer for the deadened passivity necessary to function in a capitalist factory.'

The flip side of this stereotype of passive spectatorism is the image of the spectator as hooligan. The image of the hooligan has been most recently associated with young English soccer fans running amuck at international matches, and with the violent postgame revelry that now seems to follow the winning of every Super Bowl, World Series, and Stanley Cup. Without minimizing spectator violence in our own time, it is worth noting that unruly behaviour associated with sporting contests has a long history, from the relatively common brawl in the stands to rioting that spills into the streets. A notable example of the latter occurred in Montreal in 1955, when hockey fans rioted in the stands and throughout the city to protest NHL president Clarence Campbell's decision to suspend their idol, Maurice 'Rocket' Richard. This outburst could be explained as a function of the violence that hockey itself celebrates, but it also seems clear that it was connected to the deeper resentment that French-speaking Quebeckers felt toward the anglophone elite. So, what are we to make of hooliganism, once we are through denouncing it?

The problem with the prevailing imagery of the sport fan as either 'cultural dope' or hooligan is that it portrays spectators – especially those of working class origins – either as mindless innocents sucking at the pleasurable teat of commodified leisure, or as nihilistic rowdies spawned and then forsaken by an uncaring capitalist system. This double-sided proposition oversimplifies the complex relationship between the sporting audience and the larger social and economic system. It also closes down a broad range of questions that merit the attention of sport historians. Who were and are the spectators? What racial, gender, and class issues have been associated with the sporting audience? How have audiences changed over time? How have they behaved? How were they expected to behave? Who did they cheer for? What was their contribution to the cult of the sporting hero? And, finally, to what extent has sport spectatorism contributed to the dilution of radical working-class consciousness and to the weakening of leftist politics in twentieth-century Canada? Canadian sport historians have paid remarkably little attention to these questions. In this chapter I present a historical analysis of the Canadian sporting audience from the mid-nineteenth century to the present, in the hope of providing preliminary answers to some of these questions.

Early Sport Audiences

The role of audiences in the larger universe of sporting competition, and the political, economic, and social functions associated with the sporting crowd, are issues that can be explored across cultures and across time. From ancient Rome, where 50,000 or more spectators would jam the Coliseum and the Circus Maximus for chariot races and gladiatorial contests, to football and baseball games in our own time at Toronto's Skydome and Vancouver's B.C. Place, the excitement of the crowd has revealed the elemental passion that sport can touch in the larger population. The appeal of sport has always extended beyond the participants themselves. Moreover, as audiences cheer on their heroes they intensify the meaning associated with sporting matches and spur athletes to greater levels of achievement. In this sense, audiences have contributed as much to sporting culture as have the athletes themselves. It is also true that audiences connect sport to larger social and political realities. According to Allen Guttmann, in Rome 'sports became a mechanism for the expression, and also for the manipulation, of popular opinion.' With some modification, one could say the same of sport in contemporary Canada. Yet this emphasis on the universal characteristics of the sporting audience obscures the particular historical context in which spectatorism has developed in Canada over the past century and a half.

Although an audience was important to many of the sporting activities in early Canada's rural and pre-industrial environment, the irregular scheduling of events and the scattered nature of the rural population served to limit the number of people involved as spectators. The transition to an urban, organized sporting system in the middle of the nineteenth century heightened the importance of spectators. I have already discussed the debate over the social purposes that this new sporting culture was supposed to serve. There was a similar debate over the nature and appropriate behaviour of the sporting audience. For those urban sportsmen who were committed to the amateur ideal, and who played in the protected environment of private athletic clubs, audiences were of secondary importance. Those who watched, moreover, were expected to behave in a quiet and respectable manner. One early cricket manual noted that 'it is always a proper courtesy, and tends to the popularity of this noble exercise, to allow any respectable strangers to come on the ground to witness either play or practice; but it is always good policy, likewise to have it understood by the visitors that it is a privilege, not a right.' Because the objective of sport was to compete to the best of one's abilities in a manner becoming to a 'gentleman,' and not simply to win at all costs, it would have been unseemly for audiences to cheer wildly for their favourites. Moreover, for bourgeois sportsmen at mid-century a game of cricket was usually contained within a larger social ritual that included a postgame meal, the awarding of the game ball to the winning side, formal toasts to one's opponents, and perhaps even a dance.

But games could be exciting, and as team sports became popular among the working class in the third quarter of the nineteenth century, the nature of the audience changed dramatically. The commitment to winning that accompanied the rise of professionalism and the involvement of the working class 'meant a tendency to stretch the boundaries of acceptable behaviour' among athletes and spectators alike. This was especially true of the supporters of the Montreal Shamrocks lacrosse team in the 1870s; according to Alan Metcalfe, their unwavering, raucous, and parti-

san support made them Canada's first 'modern spectators.' At championship matches, the Shamrocks drew 8,000
or more partisan fans, 'who entered freely into the game,
infringing on the play, hurling abuse at the officials and
opposing players.' Some might quibble with the choice of
the Shamrocks as the first modern spectators, given that
similar behaviour was evident among the supporters of
baseball clubs in Ontario and the Maritimes around the
same time; yet the essential point is indisputable. Strong
class, ethnic, denominational, and inter-urban rivalries were
developing on urban sporting grounds at the time, and
gambling was making victory a matter of increasing importance; as a result, sporting audiences were beginning to
flout bourgeois standards of spectator propriety, thereby
inviting the wrath of the sporting gentleman.

Civilizing Spectators

Sociologists Eric Dunning and Chris Rojek have recently
applied Norbert Elias's notion of a 'civilizing process' to
sport, arguing that modern sport accepts a 'relatively low
level of tolerated violence,' especially when compared with
earlier blood sports and the brutality of folk football and
bare-knuckle prizefighting. This 'civilizing process' is evident in attempts to discipline public audiences of all kinds,
especially those attending theatrical events. By our standards, nineteenth-century theatre audiences were unruly
and undisciplined, registering their approval of performances with shouts of encouragement, and at times pelt-
ing those on stage with fruits and vegetables to register
their dissatisfaction. According to Lawrence Levine, theatre in the nineteenth century was 'one of those houses of
refuge ... where the normative restrictions of the society
were relaxed and both players and audience were allowed
"to act themselves" with much less inner and outer restraint than prevailed in society.' Late-nineteenth-century
reformers employed a number of different techniques to

discipline public audiences. Discouraged by their failure to lift lower-class patrons to their own standards of respectability, they moved to dissociate 'highbrow and lowbrow' entertainments: on the highbrow side stood legitimate theatre, which included drama and stage plays; the lowbrow slapstick, acrobatic, and equestrian acts that had been integral to drama in nineteenth-century theatres were now consigned to vaudeville theatres, burlesque houses, and the circus. In the years since, theatregoers of all sorts have internalized standards of discipline that have made the freedom of action evident in nineteenth-century audiences a thing of the past. In today's movie houses, we threaten to breach conventional standards simply by rattling a popcorn bag too loudly.

Given how unruly sporting crowds could be, it is hardly surprising that social reformers attempted to discipline spectators at the football pitch, the hockey rink, and the baseball field. Fears of class disorder and violence lurked behind the nineteenth-century impulse to control crowds. In a society where class, ethnic, and denominational antagonism occasionally spilled over into election riots, and where working-class traditions of 'rough justice' such as whitecapping and the charivari carried more than a hint of violence, and where workers often marched in public processions to assert the rights of labour and to oppose injustice, civic authorities found crowds of any sort unnerving.

Moreover, in a baseball or lacrosse audience one found a ritualistic representation and replication of the existing social order, replete with all its tensions. Civic leaders, members of the press, and those wealthy enough to pay for seating observed the match from an elevated grandstand or from spaces reserved for those in private carriages or barouches. The rest of the crowd, youthful, boisterous, quite often drunk, and sometimes with money riding on the outcome, ringed the edges of the field, restrained by ropes but pressing ever closer to the game. And on the field itself were the players, who were required by the mar-

ket relationship between owners and workers and by the
demands of skilful production to play in an orderly manner, but whose teams often reflected antagonistic allegiances and rivalries rooted in class, race, and ethnic dif-
ferences and in urban boosterism.

And at the centre of all this stood the arbiter of fair
play, the referee or umpire, sport's equivalent of law and
just authority. Warren Goldstein has observed that in the
new team sports there was an inherent tension between
the notion of manly self-restraint and the excitement that
games produced. Those who promoted sport and codified
its rules recognized that players and audiences might lose
control in the heat of the fray and that disinterested judges
were therefore required. Usually the right to appeal to the
referee fell to the team captain, whose authority replicated
that of an elected representative in the wider political order. In many ways the umpire was the most important
figure in the game, for once his impartiality was called
into question the match lost its meaning and spectator
and player violence became more likely. Lapses in judg-
ment could be tolerated, but not corruption. Unfortunately
for those social reformers who promoted sport as a way of
winning the masses to the existing system, and who en-
dorsed the mythology of the democratic field of play, umpires were corruptible. Charges that umpires had been
bought by gamblers, or that they favoured the home team
in interurban matches, were commonplace before the First
World War. Behaviour of this sort blatantly contradicted
the message that bourgeois sport reformers wished to com-
municate to players, and through the audience to society
at large.

The 'Lady' Fan

Where in this elaborate ritual were women? For much of
the nineteenth century, women were a minute part of the
audience at baseball, hockey, lacrosse, and rugby games.

Those who did attend were usually accompanied by a male escort and sat in the grandstand away from the patrons with rush tickets. Most women avoided attending altogether, fearing that their reputations would be damaged if they patronized sports associated with gambling, alcoholism, tobacco chewing, smoking, and other forms of questionable behaviour. In fact, female patronage may have actually declined as sport became increasingly popular with workingmen. 'When photographs of the crowd show men in caps more numerous than men in hats,' Allen Guttmann has observed, 'few women are to be seen.' This was true not only for middle-class women, but also for young working girls, who might have been expected to follow their fathers and brothers to the sporting diamond, but who did not. Instead, as Kathy Peiss has demonstrated, men and women of the working class experienced leisure in different ways. At the end of the nineteenth century the young working woman's pursuit of leisure led not to the stadium but rather to other new forms of commercialized entertainment such as dance halls, amusement parks, excursion boats, and vaudeville theatres.

Thus, for the astute businessman who considered it advantageous to make sport respectable, luring women to the park became an important objective. In their attempts to 'civilize' sporting culture, promoters constructed an idealized image of the 'lady' spectator with the assistance of the middle-class press. Sporting journalists suggested that the presence of 'ladies' would purify the moral atmosphere, inspire men to behave respectably, and restrain the 'unregulated passions' that might otherwise be released involuntarily in the excitement of the moment. Leaving aside the sexual divisions inherent in all this (i.e., the assumptions that were being made about masculine excitability and female passionlessness), it is clear that women were meant to serve as 'agents of control' and to advertise the respectability of popular sporting events as a form of mass entertainment. Not surprisingly, women were usually admitted to the park free of charge as long as they were accompanied by an escort. Another inducement for female attendance was the establishment of 'ladies' days,' which suggested that a woman would find a number of her sisters in the stands. Even so, the attendance of women at professional sporting matches lagged significantly until about the turn of the century. However, as professional sport gained legitimacy in the years before the First World War, and as women became increasingly involved in sporting life as participants, playing team sports and riding bicycles, they began attending sporting contests in greater numbers.

Sporting Consumers and the Cult of the Hero

The First World War marked a point of transition from an economy focused on production to one increasingly dedicated to consumption. Having shed its reputation for rowdiness, and having assumed a new legitimacy as a pleasurable mass leisure pursuit, sport in the interwar years quickly became one of the most important elements of Canadian popular culture. Sport's growing prominence in Canadian life was related in particular to the greater attention given to sport in the daily press. Expanded newspaper coverage and early experiments in radio broadcasting helped create a new gallery of sporting idols – especially baseball and hockey players – and advertised sport to the general public as heroic endeavour. Baseball and hockey dominated interwar sporting coverage. That being said, the sports pages carried reports on many other significant events, including the Olympic Games, professional boxing championships, intercollegiate competitions, Grey Cup football, and the triumphs of the Edmonton Grads over Canadian and American competition. In short, the sporting press offered Canadians a multiplicity of overlapping allegiances, some local, some regional, some national, and some continental.

For example, the prominence of baseball in newspapers during the 1920s and 1930s revealed the strength of the game at the grass roots level in Canada while also underscoring the influence that the United States was now exerting on Canadian culture. American cultural and economic influence increased in the 1920s as Canada began to distance itself from Great Britain as part of its commitment to independent nation status, and opened its doors to American capital investment. It is hardly surprising, then, that Canadians were affected by the universalization of the American baseball hero. Canadians read about American baseball stars daily, listened to major league games on radio, and watched theatre newsreels that showed players in action. Of all the baseball heroes of the day, none was more popular among Canadians than George Herman 'Babe' Ruth of the New York Yankees. A product of the rough-and-tumble Baltimore waterfront who had spent much of his childhood in a reform school for incorrigible youth, Ruth was the supreme hero of that hedonistic age. Two decades earlier, his gluttonous appetite and sexual exploits would likely have been decried by those who worried about baseball's disreputable character. By the 1920s, however, sport was more about pleasurable consumption than proper manners.

Some complained that when Canadians 'bowed down to Babe Ruth,' they were ensuring Canada's submission to the 'American empire.' However, pro hockey supplied Canadians with home-grown heroes and a sporting identity of their own. Most Canadians think of hockey as 'our' game, and see our hockey heroes as representations of who we are. Our NHL teams affirm this in their nicknames: we are the Maple Leafs, les Canadiens, l'Habitants, and the Canucks. Indeed, as Bruce Kidd has so eloquently written, 'hockey is the Canadian metaphor, the rink a symbol of this country's vast stretches of water and wilderness, its extremes of climate, the player a symbol of our struggle to civilize such a land ... In a land so inescapably and

inhospitably cold, hockey is the dance of life, an affirmation that despite the deathly chill of winter we are alive.'
While baseball evokes the bucolic warmth of languid summer nights and tranquil 'fields of dreams' carved out of
cornfields, hockey conjures up the rugged Canadian shield,
snow-swept prairies, and a hardscrabble existence. Yet as
Gruneau and Whitson point out, the myth that hockey has
been our way of adapting to our harsh environment and
climate should not obscure the fact that the development
of the game has long been associated with struggles between men and women, social classes, regions, races, and
ethnic groups.

During the especially dark winters of the Depression,
the radio helped affirm hockey's national mystique. Live
hockey broadcasting had first been tried in the early 1920s,
but the glory days of hockey on the airwaves began in
November 1931, with Foster Hewitt's first broadcast from
the gondola in the Leafs' new arena, Maple Leaf Gardens.
By 1933, Canadians from coast to coast were huddling
around their radio receivers on Saturday evenings listening to *Hockey Night in Canada* on a nationwide network of
twenty stations. Hewitt's high-pitched voice and unique
broadcasting style captured and even intensified the excitement on the ice, and listeners rode his patented 'he
shoots ... he scores ...!' to the heights of elation or the
depths of depression. In Quebec, French-language radio
broadcasts of Montreal games were a staple of Québécois
culture, and helped consolidate the rivalry between the
Maple Leafs and Les Canadiens – that continues to this
day.

The hockey heroes of the interwar period personified
the grace, the speed, and the rugged masculinity of the
game; they also reflected the violent undercurrents that
have plagued hockey throughout its history. Eddie Shore,
a defenseman for the Boston Bruins from 1926 to 1940,
embodied all of these characteristics, and became, in Wayne
Simpson's words, 'the NHL's first major marketing phe-

nomenon.' Though a four-time winner of the Hart trophy for the league's most valuable player, and a seven-time first-team All Star, Shore is remembered more for his physical play, which bordered at times on the brutal. Shore's reputation as a 'vicious marauder' was magnified in 1933 when, with a brutal check from behind, he ended the career of Ace Bailey of the Toronto Maple Leafs. Another hockey idol of the interwar years was Lionel 'Big Train' Conacher, voted Canada's greatest athlete of the half-century. Besides being a star on the ice, Conacher played on the Toronto Argonauts Grey Cup championship team in 1921, played baseball for the Toronto Maple Leafs of the International League, was a Canadian light-heavyweight boxing champion, and was at home on the lacrosse and soccer fields. Lionel's brother Charlie starred for the Toronto Maple Leafs, playing on the noted Kid Line with Joe Primeau and Harvey 'Busher' Jackson. Quebeckers had their own heroes, like Georges Vezina (the trophy for the league's best goaltender was named after him), Aurel Joliat, a feisty and speedy left winger, and the incomparable Howie Morenz. Between them, Morenz and Joliat won four Hart Trophies, scored 540 goals, and led the Canadiens to three Stanley Cups. In 1950 a Canadian press poll named Morenz the greatest hockey player of the half-century. Morenz and Joliat were to the interwar period what Rocket Richard and Jean Beliveau would become in the two decades after the Second World War.

Although the national media's focus on the NHL meant that it was concentrating on the two largest metropolitan centres in the country, other sports spawned other heroes from across the country. Vancouver's Percy Williams won gold medals in the 100 and 200 metres at the 1928 Olympics and shattered the world record in the 100 metres in 1930. Amateur golfer Sandy Somerville from London, Ontario, won six Canadian amateur golf titles and captured the U.S. Amateur in 1932. Long-distance runner Johnny Miles from Sydney Mines was a two-time winner of the Boston Marathon and a member of the 1928 and 1932 Canadian Olympic teams. Canadian boxers were often in the limelight as well. Between 1927 and 1935, boxing consistently ranked third among all sports in the amount of coverage by major urban dailies. Irish-born Jimmy McLarnin was one of the era's elite welterweights, fighting out of New York under the watchful eye of Madison Square Garden's promoter Tex Rickard. McLarnin's thirty-fight career attracted over a half a million fans and gate receipts of more than $2,000,000. Nova Scotian heavyweight Sam Langford, nicknamed 'the Boston Tarbaby,' was denied a chance at the world title because he was Black, but during his career fought and defeated all the important heavyweights of his day. Nat Fleischer, editor of *Ring* magazine, rated Langford the seventh-best heavyweight in boxing history.

Different explanations have been given as to why the cult of the sporting hero emerged after the First World War. In part, Canada was influenced by trends in popular culture south of the border, where, according to Roderick Nash, sporting heroes recalled the triumphant individualism of the American frontier. The sporting hero of the 1920s, Nash suggests, was one 'who provided living testimony of the power of courage, strength, and honour and of the efficacy of the self-reliant, rugged individual who seemed on the verge of becoming as irrelevant as the covered wagon.' This may or may not be true, and how much sense this explanation makes for Canada is just as uncertain. A more convincing argument ties the interwar celebration of sporting heroes to the growth of a consumer culture. During the 1920s advertisers sold not only cars, washing machines, and refrigerators, but also lifestyles: gleaming teeth, odourless breath, going to the movies, a day at the ballpark, and a round at the golf course were all just a purchase away. Sporting heroes were the idols of a consuming society and were themselves to be consumed and emulated. Consumers achieved personal satisfaction the instant they purchased a pair of sneakers, or a bathing suit, or a hockey sweater, for the act itself associated them with the heroic world of the athlete.

But what of those Canadians who lacked the resources to share in the dream of consumption, yet celebrated their sporting heroes just as passionately? How are we to understand them? Don Morrow contends that sport heroes fall short of heroism, but bear 'our projections ... in a society addicted to science and devoid ... of any sense of mystery and symbols.' This is perhaps true, but our understanding of how athletes emerged as the consummate heroes of the twentieth century remains shrouded in abstraction. Whether it is true, as Morrow and Nash suggest, that the heroes of the 1920s emerged naturally as a projection of the public's own system of values, or whether instead they were deliberately cultivated to serve the interests of the emerging capitalist order, is still unclear. What we do know is that advertisers today seek out star athletes to endorse their products, and that athletes just as eagerly seek endorsement money.

Sport and Television

During the interwar years, expanded newspaper and magazine coverage of sporting events, and radio broadcasting and advertising techniques based on new understandings of behavioural psychology, did much to extend the boundaries of the sporting audience. In the years right after the Second World War, radio still had a commanding presence. In 1955 most Canadians still experienced professional hockey, football, boxing, and baseball by listening rather than watching. Fifteen years later, however, they were watching live as Neil Armstrong set foot on the moon. In that remarkably short space of time, television had revolutionized the cultural life of most Canadians. For those close to the border and with tall enough antennas, it was easy to pick up American television stations. In the 1950s,

Canadian families would hunker down in front of their living room TV sets to watch *Ozzie and Harriet, I Love Lucy,* and *The Honeymooners.* Sport fans could catch Dizzy Dean and Buddy Blattner on the CBS's *Game of the Week,* tune in to the NFL's Sunday afternoon broadcasts, watch annual sporting events like the Kentucky Derby, the Preakness, and the Belmont Stakes, or settle down with a beer to watch boxing on Friday nights.

There is little doubt that television intensified the impact of American culture on Canadian life. When they reflect on the 1960s, most Canadians of the baby-boomer generation have stronger memories of the assassination of John F. Kennedy than of the Diefenbaker–Pearson flag debate, of Martin Luther King and the civil rights movement than of the Quiet Revolution, and of Haight-Ashbury in San Francisco than of Vancouver's Gastown. However, the Canadian television networks, especially the CBC, provided an important counterweight to American network programming. Besides public affairs programs such as *This Hour Has Seven Days,* they offered the televised hoopla surrounding Canada's Centennial celebrations and the media-inspired national love affair with a dashing young Pierre Elliott Trudeau. Canadian sporting events were equally important to the moulding of the nation's consciousness. In 1957 the CBC broadcast the Grey Cup game nationally for the first time from Vancouver. Three years later the fledgling CTV network successfully bid for the game, but its limited reach brought howls of protest from the five million or so viewers who were not served by the new network. For most of the 1960s and 1970s the two Canadian networks promoted Grey Cup Week as a truly national celebration. Under the watchful eye of CBC and CTV cameras, Canadian quarterback Russ Jackson of the Ottawa Roughriders became a home-grown sporting hero, winning three Schenley outstanding player awards. In a career that began in 1958 and ended in 1969, he was also named top Canadian player in the league four times.

The attention given to Canadian sport on television in the 1960s and 1970s created national heroes at a time when south of the border the cult of the hero was rapidly disintegrating. 'Where have you gone, Joe DiMaggio, a nation turns its lonely eyes to you,' sang Simon and Garfunkel in *The Graduate*, a hit movie that depicted a young man's disillusionment with the hypocrisy of suburban life in America. American historian Ben Rader attributes the disenchantment with sporting heroes in the 1960s and 1970s to television's dilution and trivialization of sport: 'too much hype, too many "big plays," too many extraneous sensations, and too many games.' Moreover, amidst the bitter divisiveness that accompanied the civil rights movement, the war in Vietnam, and the Watergate scandal, major sport figures in the United States came to be identified with political positions. Vince Lombardi stood for old-style Americanism and 'win at any cost'; Muhammad Ali reflected the aspirations of African Americans and refused to be drafted; Joe Namath became the Hugh Hefner of American football, and Billie Jean King the sports world's greatest advocate of militant feminism. Who were the heroes, and who the villains in all of this? And did it matter to the networks as long as they kept selling time to advertisers? For television executives, the antiheroic petulance of John McEnroe hurling insults at the line judge, the outlandish antics of Dennis Rodman, the asocial behaviour of Mike Tyson, and the perverted ambitions of Tonya Harding often make for more effective marketing than the 'up close and personal' representations of more mundane or conventional athletic lives.

Canadians seem somehow less willing to politicize their sporting heroes. Perhaps because our successes in élite-level international competition are relatively rare, our heroes tend to be understood not as representatives of particular interest groups, but rather as affirmations of our nationhood. Canadian sporting stars are presented by the media and embraced by the public as national icons; in this way they contribute significantly to the Canadian complex of national myths and symbols. This places enormous pressure on our best athletes to succeed. During the 1972 hockey series between the USSR and Canada, the nation's reputation was thought to be on the line as the NHL stars took to the ice. The NHL had for years been telling Canadians that it was the world's premier hockey league, so we expected an easy victory and were stunned by the Soviet's 7–3 victory in the opening game in Montreal. After a lacklustre 4–4 tie in the fourth game of the series, which left the Canadians a game down as they headed off to Moscow, the Canadian team was roundly booed. But Canada's bruised pride was restored when, led by Phil Esposito, Frank Mahovlich, and Paul Henderson, the Canadians won three of the final four games. Every game had been beamed back live by satellite to a breathless national audience. Henderson's series-winning goal with thirty-four seconds left has been replayed more than any other Canadian sporting moment, which demonstrates the connections between TV and nation building.

Watching the Olympics

In the postwar period, television brought much greater prominence to the Olympic Games. Like the 1972 hockey series, it dramatized the Cold War through sport. The Soviets entered the Games for the first time in Helsinki in 1952, and placed second in the medal standings to the United States. Two years later at the 1954 world hockey championships, the Russians defeated Canada's representative, the East York Lyndhursts, by a score of 7–2, and thereby put Canadians on notice that their supremacy in international hockey was in jeopardy. The entry of the Soviets into Olympic competition meant fewer medal opportunities for Canadian athletes, and because of this, medal winners like skier Anne Heggtveit (gold, 1960) and runner Bill Crothers (silver, 1964) were turned into instant heroes at home. In 1968, when skier Nancy Greene won gold and silver at the Winter Olympics, she instantly became a national celebrity. Greene has recently been named Canada's athlete of the century. It is worth noting that while women were underrepresented on the Canadian Olympic teams of the 1960s and 1970s they continued to win, proportionately, at least as many Olympic medals as their male counterparts.

At the end of the 1960s the Canadian Olympic Committee was in a difficult position. It was being pressed by national sport organizations to send larger contingents of competitors to the Games; at the same time, it was being criticized by some sectors of the media for unnecessary extravagance, especially considering Canadian athletes' lack of success. The COA approached the problem by setting tougher qualification standards for athletes and at the same time attempting to increase the amount of funding available from sources other than the federal government. In 1970 the COA created the Olympic Trust, a fundraising body stacked with private-sector corporate leaders, and initiated 'Game Plan 76' to provide financial support to national sport organizations and to athletes training for the Montreal Olympics.

Canadian television coverage for the Montreal Olympics was far greater than for any preceding Games. The Canadian networks took advantage of their host status to provide elaborate coverage of the events – especially those with Canadians involved – and to present the Games as a unifying national event. Montreal itself was presented as an example of Canada's cosmopolitanism, and of its bicultural and bilingual character. The results on the field were disappointing, however, despite Greg Joy's silver medal in the high jump. When the Games returned to North America in 1984, Canadian TV coverage was even more extensive than in 1976. This growth trend has continued into the present.

For most Canadians today, the Games exist mainly (even exclusively) on television. Naturally, the national broadcasters tend to focus on those events in which Canadians are expected to do well; this means that viewers see some sports more than others. Because the United States is so close, many Canadians are able to view the games as they are broadcast on the American networks. This allows Canadians to reflect on their national identity and on how our interests differ from other people's. How we see ourselves is shaped by how 'our' broadcasters present and represent the Games to us. Organizers of both the Montreal Games in 1976 and the Calgary Winter Olympics in 1988 displayed what they considered to be Canadian symbols in the ceremonies surrounding the Games, and television sent these images throughout Canada and the world. Calgary's image makers were intent on emphasizing the city's modernity, and on representing it as a technologically sophisticated urban centre. Its resource-based past, its history as a cow town, and its Aboriginal population could thus be understood and presented simply as an expression of its 'heritage.'

As David Whitson and Kevin Wamsley point out, many cities aspire to host the Olympics because of the metropolitan status it would bring to them. This raises important questions about the place of mass audience spectacles in the new global economy. The International Olympic Committee and representatives of the state, the corporate sector, and the media work together to ensure an audience of global proportions, while civic leaders try to fashion an image of a 'world class' city. This alliance serves the interests of the national, regional, and urban elite in the host country. Yet these interests are not necessarily compatible with those of the host city's residents. When money is poured into Olympic facilities, less is available for smaller recreation centres, libraries, and other neighbourhood amenities; the result is an erosion of important public services. In the case of Montreal, for example, the deficit the city built up from hosting the Games took a generation for taxpayers to pay down. For the networks, the developers, the corporate sponsors, and individual members of the

IOC, the Olympic extravaganza was a profitable enterprise. For the expanding international audience that watches the Games on television, and that focuses only on the athletes that won and lost, the Olympics remain an exciting, pleasurable but nonetheless fleeting ritual of athletic consumerism.

Conclusion

Over the past century and a half, the sporting audience has undergone a significant transformation. Prior to 1850, sporting audiences in Canada were limited in size, and in the case of middle-class sporting clubs were constrained by notions of gentlemanly play and an emphasis on participation rather than observation. Later, as sport transcended class barriers and came increasingly to include working people, it became more intimately connected to the market. Professionalization and capitalist promotion created a new imperative: selling sport to spectators. Increasingly, the object of sport became winning rather than building character. By the turn of the last century, those bourgeois moralists who saw sport as a way to encourage patriotism, courage, self-reliance, and fair play had begun worrying about the unruliness of spectators, and establishing discourses that attempted to discipline and control sporting audiences. By the First World War, the spectre of class, ethnic, and denominational violence that had haunted the development of the industrial capitalist order had largely vanished. As well, the debate about sport's ability to create the 'respectable' community had subsided, and given way to an acceptance of sport as commercialized mass leisure.

During the 1920s, Canada's sporting culture was influenced by the emergence of mass consumerism, which had been spurred by the shift from war to peacetime production, the mass production of household appliances, the expansion of the automobile industry, and the availability of a wide range of products that promised personal happiness and fulfilment. New advertising techniques in newspapers and magazines, and over the airwaves, were being employed to sell not only tangible goods but also a way of life. In this climate, sport became more and more commodified and professionalized, and a cult of sporting heroes developed that promoted sports such as baseball, hockey, and boxing to a public looking for new leisure opportunities. The results were dramatic: new ballparks and arenas sprang up to appeal to this expanded audience, from New York's Yankee Stadium, dubbed 'the House that Ruth Built,' to the Montreal Forum and Toronto's Maple Leaf Gardens. The latter arenas testified to the success of the NHL in selling its experiment in full-market capitalism as the epitome of sporting professionalism.

Even the Depression could not keep fans away from the park or rink. Radio expanded the audience for big-time sport to include those who were unable physically to attend; it also attracted advertisers seeking to increase sales of Gillette razors, GM automobiles, Players cigarettes, and so on. When Imperial Oil began sponsoring *Hockey Night in Canada* broadcasts, it played effectively on the NHL's reputation for superiority in hockey by telling listeners to 'always look to Imperial for the best.' As competitive sport in Canada increasingly attached itself to the market, the defenders of amateurism gradually relaxed their opposition to athletes being reimbursed for their expenses. The CFL attracted imports from the United States to help sell its new 'forward-pass' version of the game, and amateur hockey clubs began providing broken time payments (i.e., compensation for time lost from work) to its players. This is not to say that professional sport triumphed unopposed: community teams, youth and intercollegiate sport, and recreational leagues continued to provide a broad base of sporting activity, and their importance to the country's sporting heritage should not be overlooked.

After the Second World War the sporting audience was remade in the context of Cold War antagonisms and the omnipresent influence of television. The geopolitical tensions between the 'free world' and the Communist Bloc brought a new intensity to international sport and swelled Canadians' interest in both the Olympic Games and the hockey world championships. When CBC and CTV beamed, live and in colour, play-by-play action of the 1972 Canada–Russia series into Canadian homes via satellite – a remarkable technical achievement for the time – it heralded a new age of global sport competition. As Canadians entered into this 'wide world of sports,' they could follow each week the skiing success of the 'Crazy Canucks' – Dave Irwin, Dave Murray, Jim Hunter, Ken Reid, and Steve Podborski – as they moved from one European ski hill to the next; and the exploits of Canada's national soccer team as it advanced through the qualifying rounds for the 1986 World Cup.

Television has raised audience awareness of sport's international dimension. It has also affected the behaviour of fans, players, and commentators alike. All too often, in their attempts to get noticed by the cameras, Neanderthals in the stands brave forty-below temperatures with bare chests, presumably in the hope that they will be considered 'real men,' impervious to pain like their on-field compatriots. In the same way, players became media clowns, spiking balls in the end zone, creating bizarre celebration routines after scoring a touchdown, dancing over sacked quarterbacks, and declaring themselves 'number one' after a good play. All of this, as Ben Rader points out, contradicts older traditions of 'exercising the restraint called for by "good sportsmanship."'

And in the press box and the television studio, commentators are now equally likely to construct images of themselves. Howard Cosell, whom Johnny Carson once referred to as a 'legend in his own mind,' epitomized the self-absorption that led sportscasters to place themselves at the centre of sporting life. According to David Halberstam, Cosell became 'his own historian, and he footnoted himself faithfully. Every broadcast was ... filled with Howard reminding us endlessly of his own insights and his predictions that had been fulfilled.' Don Cherry, former journeyman hockey player and now colour commentator on *Hockey Night in Canada*, has been just as successful in creating an image for himself that transcends the game. Cherry's brand of 'rock 'em, sock 'em' hockey is now packaged in videos that reduce the game to an endless series of crushing bodychecks. Few who purchase hockey's answer to 'K-Tel's Greatest Hits' seem bothered that it leaves the rest of the game aside. One can only hope that hockey's artistry, speed, and grace are more important to modern consumers than this would suggest.

The emergence of Wayne Gretzky and Michael Jordan as modern-day sporting heroes suggests that fans long for sport stars who remain committed to traditions of sportsmanship and who in their performances embody the grace and beauty of sport. Gretzky and Jordan may well be the greatest players to have played their respective sports, and each has cultivated an image of humility, responsibility, and mannerliness. At the same time, each testifies to the web of relationships linking sport, television, image making, the entertainment industry, and large-scale corporate capitalism. Since retiring, both Gretzky and Jordan have moved into ownership positions in hockey and basketball. The implications of this process, in which the hero athlete becomes a role model of successful corporate capitalism, are significant and are intimately connected to the commercialization and commodification of sport over the past hundred years.

5

Bodies

As we have seen in the previous chapters, sport is about many things: about our relationship with nature and animals, about how we define respectability, about how we build allegiance to community and nation, about money and profit, and about how society creates audiences and constructs heroes. To use a hackneyed metaphor, the sporting field is a 'contested territory' where class and gender relations are continually imagined and reimagined and where conflicts abound over race, ethnicity, and denominational loyalties. At its most basic level, however, sport is about the body: how it is used, how it is imagined, how it is watched, and how it is disciplined to meet the requirements of living or to conform to social expectations. In recent years, historians of sport have become intrigued with the socially constructed discourses that have developed over time about the body and its possibilities. These discourses shape how we understand masculinity and femininity. They also connect to how society categorizes race and ethnicity, perceives sexuality and the erotic, and classifies the normal and abnormal.

Historians concerned with the body have been strongly influenced by the French social theorist Michel Foucault, whose interest in the philosophical and institutional conditions of modernity led him to draw radical new conclusions about how power has been created and deployed since the Age of Enlightenment. Foucault studied prisons, asylums, schools, and hospitals, and found that in each of these modern institutions, tortuous disciplines of regulation and surveillance were being applied in the name of rationality, reform, and social liberation. In Foucault's thought, the history of the modern world is not a story of social improvement resulting from the application of rational thought and scientific techniques; rather, it is the story of how a modern form of power was constructed that resided in knowledge itself and in the disciplined practices that came to define for us the concepts of normal, useful, and necessary. Marxists see modernity as a function of the capitalist mode of production, in which all traditions that do not serve the interests of capital are subverted; in contrast, Foucault sees the modern world as one in which power is associated with the disciplines associated with rationality.

Following Foucault, we can understand sport – like medicine, nutritionism, weight training, and physical culture – as a modern technology or discipline applied to shape the body and bring it into formal public display under the deliberating gaze of the audience. In the nineteenth century, discipline in sport focused largely on creating 'manliness' and respectability. The athletic female body was considered an aberration, and displays of it were constrained by the derisive gaze of audiences, who applied conventional moral standards that later generations identified as 'prudery.' Since then, many of the myths that once limited our full appreciation of the possibilities of the female body have been discarded or at least brought into question. Yet newer discourses that involve the body are not always as liberating as we think. In a recent study of swimming, surfing, and bathing, Douglas Booth points out that the shift from Victorian moral indignation about the revealed body, to our contemporary unashamed display of the body as an object of pleasure, has involved more than just liberation from prudish moralism. In fact, modern advertising has manipulated the 'liberated' body to create a desire for (and loathing of any deviation from) an idealized and eroticized mesomorphic sporting body. In everything from beach beauty contests to bodybuilding competitions and *Sports Illustrated*'s swimsuit issue, mass consumer culture has articulated new notions of the beautiful body, which must now be shaped by rigorous and self-imposed technologies of diet and exercise. In this sense, the body since being liberated from Victorian prudery has become subjected to the cultural technologies of consumer capitalism, which through advertising presents the body as a commodity for consumption.

Vitalism and the Symmetrical Body

According to Foucault, the new disciplines of rational inquiry and surveillance that grew out of the Enlightenment were naturally concentrated on the body and mind. This was manifestly true in the nineteenth century. Physiologists believed that the laws of human life could be understood by studying the human body scientifically, just as nature's laws could be understood by observing the natural universe in all its particularity. In medicine, a new clinical and inquiring gaze was directed into the workings of discrete parts of the body and the deepest recesses of the mind. In our own time, scientists have continued this journey into 'inner space,' probing even deeper into the complexities of the body's cellular structure and of DNA, which is the very essence of life itself. These new techniques of understanding have encouraged an emphasis on both the 'healthy body' and the healthy society, and have allowed doctors and other experts to dictate the physical and moral standards that society applies to the body.

In their discourses about the natural body and its meaning for the larger social order, Victorians adhered to the principle of 'vitalism.' This was a belief that each individual was born with a finite amount of vital energy, which had to be carefully dispensed over the life course and not wasted in acts of physical or moral dissipation. The vitalist principle was at bottom a moral one: it demanded both that the body be disciplined to ensure its health, and that behaviour be socially controlled to foster a healthy social order. Most Victorians adhered to the classical ideal of *mens sano in corpore sano* (a healthy mind in a healthy body), and believed in the symmetrical development of the body, and in maintaining an appropriate balance between physical and mental pursuits. Any imbalance stemming from too much excitement of the intellect or from immoderate cultivation of physicality was therefore unhealthy and socially undesirable. Health reformers and proponents of disciplined physical culture advocated the avoidance of gluttony, the following of a purposeful exercise regimen, and the maintaining of good personal and social hygiene. Without these things, remarked the nineteenth-century phrenologist Orson Fowler, 'man can never be that finely developed and symmetrical creature that it is his privilege to be,' nor could society reach its full potential.

Criminal Types and 'Other' Bodies

Analogies between the natural body and the body politic were central to late Victorian discourses about physical and moral degeneracy, and were connected to the preoccupation with physical measurement as a means of classifying human beings. Notions of measurement permeated nineteenth-century physical and social science. Physical anthropologists measured the cranial capacity of female and male skulls, as well as those of various 'races,' and in doing so confirmed their own assumptions that Caucasian males were superior beings. Their efforts reflected the cult of normality that had developed in the nineteenth century in lock step with probability theory and statistical science. The normal having been 'scientifically' verified, it was now possible to identify the 'abnormal' or degenerate. Degeneracy theorists, among them the Italian Cesare Lombroso and Englishmen Havelock Ellis and Henry Maudsley, were fascinated by physical 'stigmata' (deviations from the 'normal'), which they were certain made it possible to classify people as 'degenerate,' 'criminal,' 'abnormal,' or 'atypical.' For Lombroso and his followers, criminal degenerates shared certain clearly identifiable physical characteristics: beady eyes, a hawklike nose (like a bird of prey), cranial deformities, asymmetrical alignment of the facial features, drooping eyelids, and deformed teeth, as well as hairy moles, 'neurotic' fingers and toenails, deformities of the pelvis and genitalia, and malformations of the brain. Physical stigmata indicated moral imbalance and a proclivity for 'degenerate pastimes.'

For people of colour, skin pigment was generally regarded as an indication of biological and hence social inferiority. It is now generally agreed that socially constructed categorizations based on the idea of 'race' have no foundation in biology, but reside in the realm of ideology. In the Victorian era, racial theory suggested that each 'race' had evolved separately and hence was at a different stage of evolutionary development. Caucasians were considered to be at the top of the evolutionary scale, and as one travelled downward the 'lesser races' were considered to be more naïve and animal-like. For Native people the idea of the 'noble savage' suggested both a natural simplicity derived from living in harmony with nature and an inability to rise above nature's influence. Blacks were thought to be of limited intelligence and unable to overcome their passionate impulses. For Black women, this suggested immorality and loose behaviour; for Black men, it suggested a threatening sexuality. These assumptions influenced how sport was organized and played. It was believed that Native sportsmen had particular physical advantages that grew out of their race and that made it impossible to accept them as true 'amateurs'; and that African Canadians lacked the intellectual and moral refinement of 'gentlemen.' By the end of the nineteenth century these propositions had solidified into a form of sporting 'apartheid' that was an integral part of debates about respectability and rowdiness, degeneracy and regeneration, the normal and the deviant.

The 'Wounded Woman'

In her compelling treatise *The Second Sex*, feminist theorist Simone de Beauvoir drew attention to the widespread tendency to regard the male body as the norm and the female body as the 'other.' Before the First World War, doctors were unanimous in contending, to their female patients and to society at large, that the female body was deviant and problematic. This biological miscategorization provided a rationale for limiting women's involvement in the public sphere, which included competitive sport and physical activities. As Patricia Vertinsky has pointed out, the medical profession's views with respect to physical exercise for women rested on 'invidious ideological assumptions about the nature of women and the assumed entitlement to medical management of the female body among the medical establishment.'

Most practitioners regarded women as prisoners of their reproductive systems, and as predisposed to weakness, ill health, and nervous disorders. Anything that distinguished women's bodies from men's, especially the 'three mysteries' of the female life cycle – puberty, menstruation, and menopause – was considered problematic. According to Wendy Mitchinson, people in the nineteenth century looked to nature as a guide for appropriate living, and what they saw as 'natural' with respect to women was not at all flattering. Women were thought to be closer to nature and less able to escape its influence. Men's physical hardiness and supposedly superior intellect allowed them to challenge nature and triumph over it; whereas women remained prisoners of their gynaecology. Because of her reproductive organs, a woman's 'natural' social role was obviously to bear and nurture children. Curiously enough, while the Victorians lauded the idea of symmetrical and balanced development of one's physical and mental faculties, they were convinced that women – and Blacks and Native people as well – were defined by their bodies rather than their minds.

This vision of female frailty accompanied new systems of industrial capitalist production and a rigidly gendered division of labour that ascribed specific roles and characteristics to each sex. Historians such as Reekie and McCrone maintain that in Britain the ideology of 'separate spheres,' which consigned women to the domestic home environment, was fashioned by the middle class to compensate for their lack of inherited status. This emphasis on respectability and female frailty distanced middle-class women from the rough and rowdy women of the lower classes. Victorian ladies of leisure were thus not only physically frailer and weaker than men, but also less vigorous than the working-class women who toiled in their homes or in their husbands' factories. The public discourse about women's participation in sport thus focused mainly on the gender characteristics assigned to middle-class women. As Lenskyj points out, 'doctors discussed exercise only in relation to *middle class* women's reproductive health, failing to recognize that poverty, malnutrition, child abuse, wife abuse, and long hours in hazardous workplaces threatened the childbearing capacities of significantly larger numbers of girls and women' (italics mine).

The Woman as Athlete

Despite the continuing debate over how physical activity affected women's reproductive capabilities, Canadian women at the turn of the century were exercising more regularly than before. In addition, women university students – admittedly an elite – were participating in sports. They were playing volleyball, badminton, basketball, and ice hockey under rules adopted to minimize body contact and discourage a 'rough unseemly, style of play.' At the University of Toronto, the first recorded women's hockey game was played in 1901, and in 1905 a league was formed. Diploma courses in physical education for women were established in 1901 at the University of Toronto and in 1908 at McGill University. Women could also use the facilities at private clubs if they were related to or sponsored by male members. Women competed in lawn tennis, curling, and golf, as well as swimming, riding, rowing, and cycling. In 1903 a women's curling team from Quebec City defeated a men's team from Scotland, and the wife of the governor general, the Countess of Minto, sponsored a ladies' skating competition. Most of the women taking part in these activities were of the middle or upper class.

There is no doubt that the universities were an important locus for women's athletics, and that they helped to break down the barriers to women athletes, even though women continued to be judged on their appearance rather than on their athletic ability. As Kate McCrone observed in her study of sport at the Oxbridge women's colleges in Britain, university women athletes spearheaded the broader movement toward feminine autonomy and served as valuable role models for their sisters: 'Every sphere of university life women penetrated, whether it was the lecture hall, the honours examinations or the sports field, told in favour of opening up new spheres and conceding to women rights to personal and public liberty.' Women's college administrators and students were well aware of how important physical education was in the larger struggle for liberation. Careful to construct their arguments for greater access to athletics within the existing malestream discourse of symmetrical development and female frailty, they argued that sport was an important antidote to mental strain and female weakness. At the 1895 annual conference of the National Women of Canada, Dr Grace Ritchie, a well-known Canadian feminist, made an earnest plea in this vein. Ritchie noted the strain that accompanied the schol-

arly pursuits of young women. Because 'their nervous systems are apt to be overworked ... we must counteract this.
The best way ... is by giving them healthy exercise in some
form or another.'

Outside the universities, as the turn of the century
loomed, women were becoming more and more dismiss-
ive of any attempts to prescribe their physical activity. Old
photos and newspaper reports suggest that women were
playing hockey across the country by the 1890s, the first
recorded instance being a game in Ottawa in 1891. A team
photo of the Edmonton Ladies team of 1899 depicts seven
women in matching sweaters, toques, and long skirts snap-
ping on skates manufactured at the Starr Manufacturing
plant in Dartmouth, Nova Scotia. On Prince Edward Island in 1893, the local press covered a game between
married and single women hockey players. Some of these
women later joined the Alpha hockey club, formed in 1895
and widely regarded as the finest women's hockey team of
the time. Elsewhere in the Maritimes, women's baseball
teams were springing up in the wake of a month-long tour
in 1891 of the Chicago Blackstockings women's baseball
club, and the Kanenites women's hockey team from New
Glasgow was developing a reputation for spirited play. At
the same time, social reformers were beginning to recognize the benefits of physical activity for both men and
women of the lower classes, and organizations such as the
YWCA were being formed to provide healthy alternatives
to the 'evils' of working-class life. Often that meant involving women in gymnastic exercises, various physical culture
regimens, and team sports like basketball and volleyball.

But it was the bicycle that had the biggest impact on
women's physical activity. For those who could afford the
new English 'safety bicycle,' introduced in 1885, riding
was both a pleasurable physical exercise and a way of es-
caping the constraints of Victorianism. Many women joined
cycling clubs or pedalled off with friends for an afternoon
outing. Cycling affected courtship patterns, sometimes even

allowing young couples to escape their chaperones. Also, because the bicycle demanded freedom of movement, it influenced dress and fashion. Many people of the time regarded cycling as an ideal form of exercise, but some worried about its moral and physical impact. Some thought the bicycle created movements that were 'muscular and less womanly' than were appropriate, and that cycling undermined the graceful and dignified bearing of the ideal young woman. Other criticisms bordered on the sensational; for example, in Canadian medical journals in the 1890s it was debated whether riding produced not only 'a distinct orgasm in women,' but also various physical maladies and a form of bicycle 'insanity.'

In the early decades of the twentieth century, social reformers also turned their attention to the moral and physical dangers thought to accompany public swimming and bathing. Their objectives were to ensure safe, supervised, and clean water spaces for swimmers and to protect working class youth from 'the medically and morally *dirty spaces* of the inner city.' These reform initiatives were motivated by notions of civic improvement and beautification, by concerns about public health and environmental degradation, and by a desire to improve recreational opportunities for the working class; but they also led inexorably to the increased surveillance and regulation of male and female bodies. In their study of recreational swimming in Hamilton Harbour, Cruikshank and Bouchier note that civic reformers in the early twentieth century were successful in developing public beaches as an alternative to unregulated swimming off dilapidated piers and wharves, which along with some notorious boathouse shacks were thought to be hangouts for crapshooting, gambling, and other forms of vice. In contrast, public beaches were supervised, with appropriate changing facilities and clearly enforced dress regulations. At the opening of one of Hamilton's beaches in 1913, a fashion show was held featuring bathing attire that conformed to standards of personal modesty. Hamilton's continuing urban and industrial growth soon made the harbour unsafe for swimming; this led reformers to advocate public swimming pools, where the campaign for moral and physical cleanliness, and for the regulation of displayed bodies could be continued.

Women and Interwar Sport

After the First World War, women were far more visible than before in the sporting arena. However, participation was consistently low among French-Canadian women (as well as French-Canadian men), relative to their English counterparts. Even so, the 1920s and early 1930s became known as the Golden Age for women athletes as sport 'moved from the domain of the upper class in their private clubs, private schools and university contexts to the public swimming pools, hockey rinks, baseball diamonds and athletic fields.' Although not every Canadian took part in physical activity, many more women were able to do so through universities, schools, leagues, clubs, and church groups. By 1920 there were more than fifty women's baseball teams in the Toronto Playgrounds Baseball Leagues. Over the next decade, across the country, adult women found plenty of opportunities to play sports and to attend events as spectators. Businesses and private sponsors had begun supporting women's sports. Moreover, as women took part in a wider range of sports, and adopted a tougher, more aggressive style of play, newspaper and radio coverage of women's sport increased. Several women wrote women's sport columns in the interwar period, including Fanny 'Bobbie' Rosenfeld of the *Globe and Mail*, Alexandrine Gibb of the *Toronto Star*, and Myrtle Cook-McGowan of the *Montreal Star*.

In part, this new visibility for Canada's women athletes reflected the growing presence of women on the international athletic stage. In 1922 the Federation Sportive Feminine Internationale organized the first women's Olympic Games in Paris; four years later, athletes from ten nations competed in the women's Games in Gothenburg, Sweden. To encourage Canadian women's participation in international competition, Alexandrine Gibb proposed a women's organization be formed in affiliation with the AAU. The new Women's Amateur Athletic Federation (WAAF) was inaugurated in December 1926, with Frances Secord of Montreal as its first president. This body operated for more than a decade, until it was disbanded with the outbreak of the Second World War.

During the 1920s a number of women sporting heroes emerged, building their reputations out of success in international competition, and adding a different dimension to the 'cult of the hero' described earlier. The leading female athlete of the day, 'Bobbie' Rosenfeld, deserves to be remembered as one of the finest all-round Canadian athletes of the century, male or female. In the 1925 Ontario track and field championships, just a year after capturing the Toronto grass court tennis title, Rosenfeld placed first in the 200-yard dash, the 100-yard low hurdles, the running broad jump, the discus, and the shot put, and finished second in the 100-yard dash and javelin – all in one afternoon! In 1928, as one of six Canadian women at the Olympic Games in Amsterdam, she was a member of the gold medal 4 by 100-metre relay team, and in a disputed decision (in the absence of a photo finish and as determined by the American judges) placed second to American Elizabeth Robinson in the woman's 100-metre dash. Rosenfeld's accomplishments led the modest Canadian women's contingent to the overall team point title over more heavily favoured national teams such as the United States; and her own individual point total exceeded that of Percy Williams, whose gold medal victories in the 100- and 200-metre dash made him the Canadian 'hero of the Games.' When Rosenfeld and her women teammates Myrtle

Cook, Ethel Catherwood, Florence Bell, Ethel Smith, and Jean Thompson returned from Amsterdam they were met by a huge crowd of admirers at Toronto's Union Station. It seemed that a new era for Canadian sportswomen had been inaugurated.

This promise was unrealized. The Depression was accompanied by increasing hostility toward women in non-traditional roles. As unemployment rose during the early 1930s, women were accused of taking jobs away from men, and social pressure mounted to force them back into their traditional roles as wives and mothers. Female athletes were criticized in turn for their tough behaviour and unladylike attitudes. One especially misogynist columnist for the *Vancouver Sun* dismissed female athletes as 'leathery faced Amazons with flat chests and bony limbs and a walk like a knock-kneed penguin.' Within the WAAF, the 1930s witnessed ongoing tensions between a conservative wing led by Ethel Cartwright of McGill and a more forceful group that included Alex Gibb. The division between them was clearest regarding the issue of 'girl rules' and 'play days,' which placed more emphasis on mass participation than on competition. Cartwright has been described as a maternal feminist because she promoted interest in women's physical activity, but only in ways that conformed with young women's maternal sensibilities and feminine demeanour. Yet as Ernie Forbes once noted about turn-of-the-century feminists, and as Bruce Kidd reiterates in his description of the debates over feminism within the WAAF in the 1930s, maternal feminism should not be dismissed simply because of its conservatism. It can also be regarded as a tactic for bringing about change. More important than where WAAFers fit in the ideological spectrum is what they accomplished. As Kidd points out, while they were not social activists, 'rather than capitulate to the reigning definitions of "feminine," they reworked them to include the right to vigorous physical activity under their own leadership. We should not allow the advances of recent years to dim the light of their accomplishment.'

One sport that women played with a remarkable degree of competitiveness, and often before large crowds, was softball. Although some women played baseball, softball grew rapidly in popularity all across the country in the 1920s. Building on the experience gained in the Toronto Playgrounds baseball leagues during the First World War and immediately thereafter, six women's teams formed the Toronto Ladies Major Softball League in 1923. A second league, the Sunnyside Ladies League, was formed the following year. Playing out of Sunnyside Stadium on the lakefront, women's softball teams drew large numbers of fans. In 1927, 1930, and again in 1932, total season attendance for women's softball exceeded that of the Toronto Maple Leafs professional baseball club of the Triple A International League. Softball was also popular in the Maritimes and the West. In the mid-1930s, Edna Lockhart of Avonport, Nova Scotia, a fine all-round athlete who starred in softball, basketball, swimming, and bowling, played two years for Margaret R. Nabel's New York Bloomers baseball team as a pitcher and at third base. (Even today, Edna regularly exceeds three hundred triples in candlepin bowling.) Farther west, women's softball flourished on the prairies and in British Columbia, and the Saskatchewan Ladies League was probably the most competitive in the country. When chewing gum magnate P.K. Wrigley established the All American Girls Professional Baseball League (AAGPBL) in 1943, the experience that young Canadian women had amassed on Canadian ball fields made them attractive to league organizers. The league operated till 1954. About 10 per cent of its players were Canadians, two-thirds of whom came from the West. Among the most notable were Helen 'Nicki' Fox of Ardley, Alberta, Helen Callaghan of Vancouver (whose son Casey Candaele went on to play major league baseball), Gladys 'Terry' Davis of Toronto, Evelyn 'Evie' Wawryshyn of Tyndall, Manitoba, and Saskatchewan native Bonnie Baker. In the summer of 1998, the Canadian women who played in the AAGPBL were inducted into Canada's Baseball Hall of Fame in St Mary's, Ontario.

Postwar Sport for Women

During the Second World War, women's participation in
sports declined as young women entered the labour force
and the military to free men for overseas military service.
Work and the increased burdens at home in the absence
of fathers, brothers, and husbands left little time or energy
for sports. International competitions were suspended and
did not resume until 1948, when the Olympic Games re-
sumed, in London, England. After the war, rigid gender
stereotypes discouraged women from participating in sports.
While minor hockey, little league baseball, and football
were widely available for boys, similar opportunities were
not available for girls. Thus, girls might use rinks for public and figure skating, but the bulk of ice time was usually
reserved for boy's and men's hockey. Moreover, new con-
structions of fatherhood in the era of 'father knows best'
suggested that gentle, constructive paternal guidance was
needed in order to turn young boys into men. What better
setting for this mixture of father as friend, mentor, and
role model than organized sport for boys, who could learn
to emulate both their dads and their baseball, hockey and
football heroes?

Canada's most popular postwar sportswoman was Barbara Ann Scott, world women's figure-skating champion
in 1947 and European, World, and Olympic champion
the following year. Acclaimed as the epitome of Canadian
womanhood, she became an icon for thousands of young
Canadian girls. Yet as Guttmann observes, 'Scott's considerable strength was seldom noticed. *Time* wrote ecstatically
of her "peaches-and-cream complexion" and Canadian
newspapers discussed her fondness for dolls. She was not
merely likened to a doll, a Barbara Ann Scott doll was
successfully marketed in Canada.' In the 1950s a gendered
representation of sports suggested that diving, synchronized
swimming, golf, tennis, gymnastics, and figure skating were
appropriately feminine; track and field, ice hockey, base-

ball, and marathon swimming were regarded as unacceptably masculine. In 1954, when sixteen-year-old Marilyn Bell became the first person to swim across Lake Ontario, her success was considered too extraordinary for her to be viewed as a role model for women. According to Wise and Fisher, Bell quickly 'withdrew from the spotlight of marathon swimming ... went on with her education, married an American boy and became as unobtrusive as any other housewife and mother.'

With the emergence of second-wave feminism in the 1960s and 1970s, more and more Canadian women began challenging the boundaries of what was considered acceptable physical activity for women. In 1972 the Report of the Royal Commission on the Status of Women made a number of recommendations relating to sport for women and identified systemic inequalities that needed to be addressed. Women's sports in Canada were underfunded, and in addition to there being a much lower rate of participation for female athletes, women were woefully underrepresented in coaching and sports administration and at the executive levels of sport. These problems continue into the present, but as a result of equity legislation in both the United States and Canada, great advances have been made, especially in university athletic programs for women. In recent years this has resulted in a growing prominence for women in team sports, including basketball, soccer, and hockey. In 1997 the Women's National Basketball Association (WNBA) was established, and at the Winter Olympics in 1998 women's hockey was one of the sports showcased by television networks in both Canada and the United States.

Athletic Bodies in the Contemporary Age

Although more enlightened attitudes toward the athletic possibilities of the female body have emerged in the past few decades, women continue to confront assumptions about their athletic inferiority – assumptions rooted in notions of what the body should be, what discipline it should be subjected to, and what it can achieve. According to Varda Burstyn, our modern big-time sporting culture creates and reproduces an elitist, masculinist account of power and social authority that reveals itself in contemporary presentations of the athletic male body. The body aesthetics that accompany this sporting culture, she argues, venerate massive muscularity in men and suggest that power naturally coheres in maleness. The hyperdeveloped muscularity of an Arnold Schwarzenegger, of bulked up football players, and of giant basketball stars contrasts with the 'diminishment of women in sport'; smallness is more and more being taken to signify femininity. This trend toward tininess began in earnest in the 1970s, and was most evident in 1972, when 4'11, 82 pound Olga Korbut captured gold in gymnastics at the Munich Olympics. Yet this tendency toward the diminished body among women athletes carries a significant price: eating disorders, including bulimia and anorexia nervosa, exact a tremendous physical penalty on those who try to conform to images of the ideal female athlete. The diminished feminine form is associated with youth, weakness, and subordination; this contrasts dramatically with the images of power and dominance that accompany masculine muscularity.

Yet when we emphasize only this polarity of a hyperdeveloped masculinity and a minimized femininity, we are paying insufficient attention to the different 'masculinities' and 'femininities' that have superimposed themselves on the body over the past quarter-century. Assumptions about what is 'natural' have changed dramatically in that time. Gay and lesbian athletes are challenging the conventional stereotypes of masculinity and femininity; physically challenged athletes are increasingly being recognized and applauded for their athletic abilities; and the use of drugs and nutritional supplements has visibly altered both male and female sporting bodies. This suggests that the disciplines that are applied to the body in ways that construct

idealized notions of the masculine and the feminine cannot encompass the diversity of identities that make up the
world of our athletes or of those who watch them.

In the physical and intellectual construction of the body
we encounter fundamental questions relating to power,
resistance, identity construction, and ethics. The physical
body, like the body politic, is contested territory, and is
influenced by assumptions about who we are and should
be. Our bodies are as diverse as the identities we impose
on them, and resist attempts to make them conform to
homogeneous standards of the appropriate. However, according to Debra Shogan, 'like political struggles over diversity in the workplaces, legislatures, courts of law, and
communities, diversity will not be welcomed by those who
want participants to be homogenous ... If sport ethics is
not to continue to be a "powerless protest against sport,"
an important task of sport ethics will be to upset this ho-
mogeneity.'

Bodies, Class, and Status

Up to this point we have focused on how the body is impli-
cated in discussions of sexual identity and gender construction. If our bodies are 'canvases' on which we paint
our culture's values, they reveal not only our assumptions
about gender but also our class and cultural experiences.
We establish our identities by adorning our bodies, by im-
posing discipline on them, and by presenting and display-
ing them. Our Nike high-top sneakers, our form-fitting
workout clothes, the sporting caps we wear with the peak
forward or backward, and the clothes we wear at the local
golf club all point to the impact that modern consumerism has had on sport and on our sporting bodies. Yet
there is more to this than mere fashion. Our willingness to
accept or resist various forms of adornment, and to choose
other embellishments such as body piercing or tattooing,
relates to our personal values. It also relates to our class,

gender, and ethnic and historical experience. We need only conjure up the image of young Palestinians in Reeboks throwing rocks or Molotov cocktails to understand that however pervasive global capitalism is, its influence is both ambiguous and contested.

Besides this, the very sports in which we involve ourselves, or with which we identify, can reveal our social aspirations and status. According to Douglas Booth and John Loy, members of the social elite have tended to engage in sporting activities that involve a 'dignified presentation of the body.' These activities usually require a higher investment of time and money, and sometimes the employment of sporting surrogates (e.g., caddies in golf, jockeys in horseracing, native bearers or guides in hunting safaris or mountain climbing). Elite sport also often involves owning animals, as in polo and horseracing. Sports like golf, sailing, and skiing suggest an upper-class interest in activities that can be undertaken at a leisurely pace and in spaces that are relatively unbounded. As we have seen, middle-class Victorian sportsmen were attracted to team sports that promoted 'manliness,' fair play, self-restraint, and competitiveness. All of these conformed to 'the ethical imperatives and aesthetic preferences of the middle class' and were played within clearly defined spaces and with clearly defined rules of competition that denied special privilege. At the same time, these middle-class sportsmen were concerned about the rough behaviour and raw emotions that accompanied working class sport. 'Even today,' Booth and Loy write, 'the lower classes typically engage in sports that are accessible, display a degree of violence, require a large investment of physical exertion, often entail personal risk (e.g. boxing, motorcycling), and most of all provide excitement.'

Yet this taxonomy of sporting style and status is by no means rigid or immutable. Rather, the associations of particular sporting practices with particular social groupings or classes are in constant flux, which reflects the ongoing struggle to redefine class relations within an evolving capitalist social and economic order. Indeed, the very process by which capital presents sport and the lifestyles attached to it as a commodity has allowed white-collar workers and some members of the working class to penetrate sporting spaces that were once closed to them. For athletes the particular dynamics of the sporting marketplace are such that successful jockeys can become horse owners, star hockey players can become sporting magnates, and Formula One race car drivers can become idolized companions of the jet set. This is not to say that class and status have become disconnected from sporting life. As one can imagine, the audiences at truck pulls and wrestling matches are different from those at golf tournaments and tennis matches. It does mean, however, that the associations between class, status, and sporting style are more complex now than they have ever been.

Conclusion

Imagine for a moment that we could find an anthropologist or historian unfamiliar with the sporting culture of the twentieth century. Admittedly, this would be a tall order. Nevertheless, what might she conclude about its meaning? Obviously she would be interested in sport's commercial and civic objectives, and its attachment to an expanding consumer marketplace that offers for sale not only goods and services but also an approach to life. Given the extent of sport's influence and popularity, she might even think of sport as a powerful civic religion, at once reflecting and shaping social mores. But would she not also be fascinated by the important place that sport and the body have occupied over the past century in the social construction and imagining of gender roles, and in the casting of relationships between the classes?

At the beginning of the century, women's involvement in sport was strictly prescribed, and the female body shielded from the public gaze. It was believed that sport diverted the vital energy a woman needed to carry out her 'natural' responsibility of child-bearing; and medical doctors presented a complex biological argument about the frailty of the female body. It was considered unnatural, unfeminine, and unhealthy for a woman to be actively engaged in sport. Not surprisingly, in the sexual division of leisure, women were relegated to the sidelines as spectators. In sport, as so often in society as a whole, women were urged to be passive consumers of what active males produced. Not all women accepted their exclusion from an active sporting life, however, and by the end of the nineteenth century many had taken to the sporting pitch.

Nevertheless, when women did play they were usually urged to partake in activities that promoted supposedly feminine attributes such as grace, elegance, passivity, and beauty. Some of the barriers to women's participation have fallen over the years, but it is fair to say that sport remains a bastion of male authority and power. In the words of Helen Lenskyj, 'femininity in sport militates against authentic expressions of physical and mental strength; it requires artifice, a deliberate effort to convey ease, grace and charm. Masculinity in sport is less dependent upon artifice, makeup or play acting; it does not carry the same expectation that concentration or strain be concealed behind a bland, smiling mask.' Yet even in our contemporary age, in which images of the hypermasculine male physique are constantly presented in the media, in Hollywood films, and in popular pornography, and by contrast women are bombarded with images of an idealized and diminutive femininity, these stereotypes are regularly contested. As Debra Shogan points out, 'athletes, like other people, participate in a number of overlapping, conflicting disciplines that together produce a distinctive hybrid identity for each person.' The greater tolerance that now exists for those who refuse to conform to homogenous assumptions of 'masculinity' and 'femininity' suggests that the physical body continues to be a site of enduring ideological conflict and resistance.

In a similar way, the Canadian body politic has been affected by a multiplicity of identities. As we have seen, the meaning of sport varies with one's region, class, ethnicity, race, and gender. Canadians in the countryside established leisure and sporting activities that conformed to their interests, and that differed from those of the sporting culture which developed in conjunction with the newly emerging urban and industrial order. Thus, the sporting experiences of those in the hinterland were different in many ways from those in metropolitan centres. The sports that captured the interest of francophone Quebecers were not the same as the ones that were accepted and reproduced by the anglophone elite. Sport in northern communities and among aboriginal peoples has often served to maintain cultural traditions that help ensure those groups' survival. At the same time, new communications technologies and the emergence of a global economy have created what Stacey Lorentz calls a transnational 'information system' that constructs a 'world of sport' and that involves 'the entire range of ideas, attitudes, symbols, and knowledge that constitutes the common experience of sport.' Yet despite the multiplicity of sporting experiences and identities that all this implies, sport continues to be understood as an exercise in nation building. To understand the ambiguous and at times contradictory relationship between sport and the nation, we now turn to the question of sport, the state, and national identity.

6

Nation

At the Olympic Games in Atlanta in 1996, Donovan Bailey sprinted across the finish line in the 100-metre final and became, at least for the moment, the 'world's fastest human.' Bailey grabbed a Canadian flag from a willing spectator, wrapped it around his shoulders, and ran a triumphant victory lap of the stadium track. For most Canadians who watched the race, this was a stirring moment, a unifying celebration for a country that faced the possibility of separation and that had suffered through the elation and bitter disappointment of the Ben Johnson doping scandal at the 1988 Games. For the Jamaican-born Bailey, who arrived in Canada as a thirteen-year-old and later became a Canadian citizen, victory provided a chance to celebrate both his adopted country and his birthplace. 'I'm Jamaican-born,' he said in a postrace interview. 'I am also a Canadian citizen. There's no way I'm going to choose between what country I won the medal for.' Some members of the Canadian press corps grumbled that Bailey should have asserted an unalloyed allegiance to Canada; others saw his comments as an affirmation of Canada's multicultural identity. 'Canada has for decades actively encouraged its citizens to treasure their ethnicity and told them they need not abandon one identity upon taking on a new one,' wrote Christie Blatchford in the *Toronto Sun*. At the same time, she noted, 'a good many Canadian-born Canadians take great offence when those who come to our country take it to heart when

we tell them we don't expect patriotism from them, only
perhaps a measure of gratitude.'

Bailey's victory, which appealed to Canadians in so many
different ways and on so many different levels, raises questions about Canada's relationship with sport. How we understand this relationship is connected to how we view the
nation itself. According to Benedict Anderson, nations are
'imagined communities.' By this he did not mean that
they are mere illusory fabrications, but rather that they are
grounded in the assumptions of a particular time. Over
the years, Canadians have imagined their nation in various
ways, as a function of their various class, ethnic, and regional vantage points and the intellectual climate of the
time. It is important to consider how Canadians come to
conceive of the nation as a larger entity, because face-to-
face interactions between citizens are impossible on a grand
scale. In any given period of time, Canada's cultural institutions – which include the national media, the sporting
bureaucracy, and sporting events that act as unifying cultural enthusiasms – help construct the nation as a coher-
ent identity. The extent to which our understanding of
the nation can accommodate its various identities is a ba-
rometer of Canada's success and an indication of how much
allegiance it has won.

Sport, Nation, and Empire

In the period between Confederation and the First World
War, Canadians erected the social, political, economic, and
cultural infrastructure of nationhood. The most obvious
manifestation of nation building was the national policy of
John A. Macdonald's Conservative government, which involved a protective tariff, a transcontinental railway, and
the settling and subjugation of the West. On the psycho-
logical or emotional level, however, our national consciousness, or shared identity, was still clearly under construction. Early attempts to define that identity often took the
form of a romantic Anglo-Saxonism, which connected

Canada's national identity firmly to that of Great Britain and its empire. Various poets and artists celebrated the new nation in verse or on canvas. At the same time, a nationalist movement known as 'Canada First' was presenting a vision of the country that was not only exclusionist but racist. Canada Firsters such as Thomas Haliburton considered native peoples uncivilized and inferior and French Canadians a 'bar to progress'; they identified Canadians – at least those of the male variety – as 'the Northmen of the New World' and described Canada as a new nationality embracing 'the Celtic, the Norman French, the Saxon and the Swede.' Jack Bumsted contends that it was unfortunate that Canada's emerging cultural nationalism came to be identified with the Canada First movement, 'for the Canada Firsters had neither a monopoly on national sentiment nor a very attractive version of it.'

As we have seen earlier, attempts by Canadians to build national spirit on the foundations of Anglo-Saxonism extended to sport. This is hardly surprising, given Canada's place in the Empire, the sentimental attachments many Canadians had to the Old World, and the country's long-established commercial and cultural links to England. The early British games transplanted to Canada – among them cricket, rugby, soccer, curling, and golf – were thought to be character building, and to instil in young men the virtues of patriotism, self-control, fair play, and manliness. Yet for many Canadians these sports were exclusive and elitist, and lacked the appeal of North American games such as baseball, lacrosse, and ice hockey. French Canadians showed little interest in British games; for them, as for Maritimers, hockey and baseball were the predominant winter and summer sports. By the beginning of the Great War, attempts to impose notions of Anglo-Saxon imperialism through sport had been only marginally successful.

After the First World War, Canada's new self-confidence as a nation, which had been forged on the battlefields of Europe, led to a movement for Dominion status within the

British Empire. Athletic competition at the British Empire and Olympic Games became an important venue for Canadians to express their nationalist sensibilities. The new nationalism of the postwar years helped the Amateur Athletic Union of Canada further its project of building the nation through sport. Leading figures in the AAU such as Norton Crow, W.A. Hewitt, and James Merrick zealously defended the high ground of amateurism in the 1920s and early 1930s; the AAU also became increasingly preoccupied with international competition and with promoting high-performance athletics. Recognizing the prestige that success in international competition could bring, the AAU adjusted the constitution of the Canadian Olympic Association so that it became the Canadian Olympic Committee, a standing committee of the AAU. This brought it more completely under AAU control and ensured its adherence to the AAU's strict dictates concerning amateurism. Not that this would have been a huge issue in the early years of the interwar period. On many occasions, the AAU was gratified to hear some of the major international sports federations as well as the IOC make pronouncements on amateurism that fit well with its own policies. This validation from outside the country undoubtedly helped solidify the AAU's position as Canada's sporting conscience.

Having received firm support from the IOC for its policies relating to amateurism, the AAU began promoting high-performance athletics as a way of fostering Canada's national identity. This meant a new emphasis on national championships and on appropriate qualifying procedures for international competition. The AAU tried to make the selection process as fair as possible by moving national finals from city to city and by staging regional finals, from which participants could move on to the national competitions. However, Canada's geography dictated against large numbers of athletes from all parts of the country participating in national finals, no matter where they were held.

Olympic teams thus tended to be composed of athletes from the major cities, which hosted the majority of regional and national finals. Issues relating to ethnicity, class, and sex also mitigated against some Olympic aspirants. In the interwar period, French-Canadian and Aboriginal athletes were much less likely to make Canada's Olympic teams. Moreover, those who had to work for a living found it difficult or impossible to invest sufficient time and energy to participate in sport at the highest levels. They required compensation of the kind that was not permitted under AAU rules. Thus, while Olympic competition might stir the patriotism of those athletes who could afford it, for working class athletes playing for pay in the capitalist sporting environment often made more sense than maintaining amateur standing in order to play for Canada. In some ways, then, the hope of creating a sporting nation open to all had not yet been realized.

Sport and Region

It would be unwise to disregard the extent to which sport contributed to Canadian nationalism between the wars, when the foundations of a broad new national culture were being laid. At the time, Canada's Group of Seven were taking a frankly nationalist approach to art, and the CBC and National Film Board were emerging as important national forces in public broadcasting and film production. Concomitant with this, national sporting allegiances were developing across the country just as the Depression was straining loyalties, undermining faith in political leaders, and pitting the provinces against the federal government. Competitions in football and hockey leading to the Allan Cup, Stanley Cup, and Grey Cup, and Canadian successes at the Olympic Games, provided a common experience and shared identity for Canadians throughout these difficult years. The myth/symbol complex of nationalism was

further consolidated during the Second World War, when
the country confronted Naziism and Japanese militarism.
After the war, an emerging social welfare state built on a
new arrangement in Dominion/provincial relations enhanced national allegiances across the country.

Yet not all Canadians felt that they were sharing equita-
bly in the larger national order. In the Maritimes, where a
dismantling of the region's industrial base had resulted in
deindustrialization and widespread outmigration, there was
little sporting interaction with the rest of the country. Many
Maritime athletes, such as marathoner Johnny Miles, who
complained bitterly that he could not make a living in
Cape Breton and would have to move away, shared the
sense of betrayal and alienation that energized the interwar Maritime Rights protest. And those Maritime athletes
who did qualify to represent the country in international
competition complained of being discriminated against by
national team coaches and officials. When not even one
player from the 1935 Allan Cup–winning Halifax Wolver-
ines was included on the 1936 Olympic hockey team, these
feelings of regional alienation were reinforced. Moreover,
without a national hockey or football franchise the region
could experience the sporting rivalries in the rest of the
country only vicariously. And the success of the Caledonia
Rugby Club, perennial eastern Canadian rugby champions
in the 1930s, could not conjure up a sense of full participation in the national sporting order, given that an Ameri-
can-style game was developing in much of the rest of the
country. In many respects, Maritimers' sporting ties with
New England were stronger than they were with the rest of
Canada. Touring baseball teams from the United States,
especially those made up of players from the American
Negro leagues, regularly barnstormed through the region,
and Maritime clubs occasionally returned the favour. In
contrast, when the Montreal Dow club played a couple of
games in the region in 1936, it marked the only visit to

the Maritimes by a baseball team from another Canadian province between the turn of the century and the Second World War.

The outbreak of war did much to soothe Maritimers' sense of alienation. Halifax became the most important staging port for the overseas war effort and the Battle of the Atlantic, and this reinforced the flush of patriotism that accompanied the conflict. And as Canadians from across the country came through the city on their way overseas, many of Canada's best athletes were temporarily stationed there. Initially there had been some debate as to whether sport should be carried on during the war, but it was soon recognized that sport helped keep up morale among military personnel and those on the homefront as well. Maritimers were delighted to be able to watch Canadian major league baseball stars such as Phil Marchildon, Dick Fowler, and Joe Krakauskas, and NHL luminaries Gaye Stewart, Bob Goldham, and Bob Dill, as they played alongside local sporting heroes on community ball diamonds and hockey rinks. After the war, improvements in broadcasting communication, and national radio and television coverage of sporting events, contributed further to the Maritimers' sense that they were part of the broader sporting nation. Today Maritimers are especially proud that they are the permanent venue for the CIAU basketball championships, and each year the Atlantic Bowl football game plays to sell-out crowds in Halifax. Both these events contribute to Maritimers' pride in their region and help secure its allegiance to the nation as a whole.

The Postwar Sporting State

The relationship between national policy and fitness and sport is highly visible in contemporary Canada, yet the state's interest in fitness and sport is by no means new. The military has always seen the advantages of keeping citizens fit, and all levels of government have always shown an interest in regulating recreational activities. During the First World War, military leaders fully realized how useful sport was in preparing troops both physically and mentally for battle, in boosting morale, and in providing rest and rehabilitation to troops returning from the front lines. For example, in 1918 the Dominion Day athletic championships of the Canadian Corps in France were held as the culmination of a number of qualifying events in which 70,000 soldier athletes took part. The individual exploits of the participants were publicized alongside the honour rolls of Ypres, the Somme, Vimy Ridge, and Passchendaele. Sport was thus not only a moral equivalent of war – it had become part of war itself.

In wartime the need for physically fit recruits sometimes encouraged government legislation, but the state's commitment to sport was temporary and hardly extensive until after the Second World War. During the Second World War, in 1943, the Canadian government passed the National Fitness Act, which parcelled out federal money to the provinces for fitness and recreation programs. Unfortunately, it was unclear from the act what the term physical fitness meant, and the subsequent narrow interpretation by the Justice Department created a situation that limited the funds available and how they could be used. As a result, the provinces expressed little interest in the program. Quebec immediately opted out, claiming that the federal grants infringed upon provincial jurisdiction. Ontario did not join until 1949, a year after New Brunswick, and Prince Edward Island participated only from 1945 to 1952.

The National Fitness Act was eventually repealed in 1954, but the foundations for an active presence by the federal government in the area of sport had been laid. The Canadian Sports Advisory Council and the Canadian Association for Health, Physical Education and Recreation were already lobbying the government, claiming that the declining health of Canadians cried out for a national fitness policy. Sporting organizations also drew attention to Canada's increasingly poor performances abroad, especially in hockey, arguing that sport was connected to Canada's international prestige. In the Cold War era, sport was regarded as an important albeit informal component of Canada's foreign policy. A widely circulated 1958 brief from the Canadian Sports Advisory Council emphasized that sport was important to national defence, economic development, culture, and health. The Conservative government of John Diefenbaker was eventually persuaded of the virtues of sport nationalism and took steps to promote fitness and amateur sport across the country. Sport thus became an important element in the new social welfare state, which also provided Canadians with hospital insurance and medicare benefits, supported high culture and the arts, and increased funding for postsecondary education.

The passing of Bill C-131, *An Act to Promote Fitness and Amateur Sport,* in September 1961 marked the beginning of massive federal funding of programs to raise Canada's profile in international sport as a form of nation building. The bill promoted fitness and amateur sport at all levels and allowed the government to fund research, bursaries and fellowships, conferences, and coaching, as well as practically any other support required. Bill C-131 created the National Advisory Council on Fitness and Amateur Sport (NAC), whose members were knowledgeable in the areas of physical fitness, recreation, and sport. In 1962, provision was made to create full-time civil service positions under the Directorate of Fitness and Amateur Sport. An annual grant to sport organizations of $5 million was authorized, to be administered by the Department of National Health and Welfare. One million dollars was allocated the first year; a further $1 million was added each year thereafter until the $5 million level was reached in 1966–67. This bill marked a shift toward the idea that sport – associated as it was with the nation's health and welfare – was a federal issue and should be approached as a component of the social welfare state. Until then, sport had been considered the exclusive province of volunteers operating within various local, regional, and national sports organizations (NSOs).

In the 1960s and 1970s, the federal government also set out to create a national infrastructure for sport and to promote physical fitness in the general population. Two initiatives, the Canada Games and the ParticipAction program, were especially successful. The Canada Games, conceived as a way to develop athletes from across the nation and to encourage national unity, were introduced in the heady spirit of Canada's centennial celebrations. The first Canada Games were held in 1967 in Quebec City, for obvious political reasons. These Games took up the motto 'Unity through Sport' and attracted 1,500 athletes from every province and territory. In the early 1970s the federal government introduced the national ParticipAction program with the goal of getting more Canadians more physically active. Canadians were urged to stand rather than sit, walk rather than stand, and run rather than walk. The physically challenged were encouraged to become active as well, and in the years to come athletes such as Terry Fox and Rick Hansen became national heroes. For the developmentally challenged, competitions such as the Special Olympics were organized, and were supported across the country.

These initiatives underscored the state's interest in physical fitness, in promoting sporting activity for all citizens, and in fostering national unity. The government's approach to allocating resources suggests, however, that it was emphasizing high-performance sport. During the 1960s, activities such the world hockey championships, the Pan-Am Games, and the development of major sporting facilities associated with élite sport represented 34 per cent of allocated funds. National grants to various organizations for a variety of projects amounted to 22 per cent. Federal–provincial cost sharing programs took another 20 per cent, while scholarships, fellowships, and bursaries in physical education, recreation, and research received 11 per cent. The Canada Games received 8 per cent, and information programs ate up the remaining 5 per cent.

During the 1970s the federal government became even more committed to high-performance sport. The Task Force on Amateur Sport, which Prime Minister Pierre Elliott Trudeau struck in 1968, focused on Canada's involvement in international sport. The report was commissioned, in large measure, because of Canada's continuing lack of success in international sport, with the Olympic Games being the most obvious example of failure. Sport Canada, a national nonprofit corporation established to provide sport organizations with a centralized meeting place (and access to the government), was one result of the task force's recommendations. In 1977 another government working paper suggested that amateur sport organizations should work toward a fifty–fifty funding split between government and the private sector, and advocated a more rationalized, professional business model for amateur sport organizations across the country. During the 1980s, Canadian amateur sport officials accelerated their move toward a more business-oriented management model for their organizations. Government studies encouraged this transition by suggesting that federal funding would soon be made contingent on this type of reform. Those who governed elite amateur sport began taking a more corporate approach in the expectation that this would lead not only to more efficient management but also to greater success in international competition.

Canadian successes at the 1984 Olympic Games seemed to confirm the wisdom of this new approach. For the first time in more than a decade, Canadian athletes won many medals, including gold. The media pointed out that many of the world's best athletes were missing from the Games because of a boycott led by the Soviet Union; even so, Canadian success spurred hopes for more of the same in future competitions. Another government paper, released in 1988, went so far as to suggest that Canada should aim to place a specific number of athletes in the top ranks at the next Olympics. The successes of Canadian athletes at the international level had immediate benefits and contributed to national unity; in contrast, sport and fitness programs for the general population provided few dramatic results. Government financial support for amateur (Olympic) sport thus reached its zenith while promotion of mass sport and fitness was being relegated to secondary status within the Ministry of Fitness and Amateur Sport.

Sprinters, Steroids, and Subsidies

The archetypical example of the success of Canada's system for creating Olympic medal-winning athletes was, at least for a few days in 1988, sprinter Ben Johnson. Of course, his positive test for a banned substance led to several years of Canadian soul-searching with respect to Olympic sport. Justice Charles Dubin presided over a Royal Commission into the use of banned substances in sport. In June 1990 his *Report of the Commission of Inquiry into the Use of Drugs and Other Banned Practices Intended to Increase Athletic Performance* was tabled in House of Commons. The Dubin Report revealed that banned substances were well known and widely used in Canada's community of athletes, coaches, and officials. Some of the blame for the situation was placed on Canada's system for developing athletes. Obviously, steroid use in sport is also connected to the growing social acceptability of drug use in society as a whole. Reliance on banned substances also suggests how much pressure athletes face to perform well at élite levels, and how much is at stake financially in international sports. The response of the federal government, which itself contributed to the problem by emphasizing the importance of high-performance athletics, was to establish a new Canadian antidoping organization that would coordinate and

administer future antidoping initiatives. Canada now has
the most stringent drug-testing procedures of any international sporting nation.

Not surprisingly, after the Dubin Report was released,
the federal government's support for elite amateur sport
changed dramatically. The heady language of producing
certain numbers of top-ranked athletes in certain sports
disappeared. Indeed, in the early 1990s financial restraints
and the government's decision to become more fiscally
responsible led to the Ministry of Fitness and Amateur
Sport being swallowed by the newly created Ministry of
National Heritage. This demotion reflected the federal
government's desire to cut costs and to have national sporting organizations assume more responsibility for raising
their own funds. Having lost its status as a ministry, Fitness
and Amateur Sport also faced a significant reduction in
federal grants, which till then had been divided among
national sport organizations through Sport Canada. In recent years this has meant a new emphasis on the corporate
sponsorship of athletics and on fundraising in the private
sector. Despite the state's commitment in principle to fitness and healthy lifestyles – as evidenced by the continuing stress on ParticipAction – and on sporting activities
that assert (albeit often in superficial ways) Canada's
multicultural character, federal financial support for sport
and recreation has suffered amid demands for fiscal
responsibility.

Sport and Multiculturalism

That Canada is a multicultural nation is one of the fundamental propositions of contemporary discourse. Most Canadians today would agree that it is better to recognize the
diversity of Canadians and their overlapping identities and
allegiances, than to impose a uniform sense of identity on
them. It follows that the relationship between sport, identity, and nationalism is multifaceted and multilayered. The

persuasiveness of the idea of multiculturalism is such that it has become generally accepted as common sense, as the way things are and presumably should be. At the same time, it is important to recognize that multiculturalism is also a political strategy employed to neutralize conflict and dissent, and a means for the state to legitimize itself. Just as the federal government promoted bilingualism and biculturalism in the 1960s and 1970s as a response to Quebec nationalism, it has now committed itself to multiculturalism as a means of securing support from immigrant groups and of responding to the claims of Aboriginal peoples for social and economic justice.

Federal government assistance for sport among aboriginal peoples began in earnest during the 1970s, a decade that according to Vicky Paraschak represented a Golden Age for Native sport. In 1970 the Trudeau government provided financial support for the inaugural Arctic Winter Games, held in Yellowknife for Native athletes living north of the 60th parallel. These biennial Games were designed to provide sporting opportunities and competition to a 'disadvantaged' region, and to prepare Native people for involvement in elite competition at the national level. The following year, acting on the principles enshrined in a Fitness and Amateur Sport policy document titled *A Proposed Sports Policy for Canadians*, the Trudeau government introduced the Native Sport and Recreation Program. This program revealed the government's desire to 'devote special attention to the less fortunate regions and classes of people in the country.' Its specific objectives were to help native people develop leadership skills in recreation program management, and to raise performance levels among native athletes so that they could compete in national competitions.

Throughout the 1970s, Native leaders across the country drew on this support to create a sport system that encouraged native solidarity and cultural expression, in opposition to the federal government's desire to assimilate

Native athletes into the larger Canadian sport edifice. According to Paraschak, the Native Sport and Recreation Program involved both 'patterns of reproduction' and 'patterns of resistance.' From their Eurocentric perspective, federal government officials believed that Euro-Canadian sports were 'the "natural" form of legitimate physical activities.' Native participants embraced these sports and thus reproduced Euro-Canadian sports such as hockey, fastball, bowling, track and field, boxing, basketball, and curling; yet they also sometimes included in their competitions culturally distinct activities such as powwows, music performances, and cultural traditions workshops. Native leaders wanted to use the Native Sport and Recreation Program to develop a segregated sport system, one that would enhance and promote their own culture instead of turning out elite athletes for national competition. In opposition to the assimilationist intentions of the government, they wanted to develop representative but separate Native teams that would be included in major national and international competitions. To them, this was a way of promoting the interests of the Native people.

These conflicting goals imperilled the Native Sport and Recreation Program. In 1976, Iona Campagnolo became Minister of State for Fitness and Amateur Sport. During her three-year term she began to express the government's discomfort with the autonomy that native communities had carved out for themselves under the existing support program. In 1978 she made it clear to Native leaders that they would have to assimilate their sport programs with Fitness and Amateur sport or lose their funding: 'If you think that what I am trying to do is assimilate you, you are right ... This does not mean cultural assimilation of the Indian people. It simply means that you get into the mainstream and compete like everyone else.' When Native leaders refused to capitulate to this assimilationist policy, and continued to argue instead for a sporting policy informed by broader cultural concerns, the federal government withdrew its support. In 1981 the Support Program for Native Peoples was discontinued.

Ever since, Aboriginal peoples have been developing self-directed sport and recreation programs that are suited to their own needs and that draw from their own traditions. In various conferences such as the ones held in the Northwest Territories in 1983, 1991, and 1996, serious attempts have been made to involve participants in the decision-making and planning process. In 1988, J. Wilton Littlechild, an Aboriginal rights advocate, began organizing the first North American Indigenous Games. The first of these games were held in Edmonton in 1990, and attracted over 3,000 athletes from across North America. They have since become a regular feature of Native sporting life. More recently, attempts have been made to revive the Arctic Winter Games and to involve indigenous peoples from Siberia, Alaska, Greenland, and the Northwest Territories in friendly competition.

Conclusion

The experience of Native peoples and sport in recent years raises important questions about sport as a nation-building exercise, and about whose perceptions of the sporting nation should take precedence. Over the years, Canadian sport has been a collective exercise. It has involved Canadians from all regions; it has taken place in both the countryside and the city; and it has included professional and elite competitions as well as local and community-based sport. It has often involved struggle, conflict, and resistance, as well as attempts to exercise social control and maintain hegemonic authority. At times sport has involved struggles for liberation, and contributed to self-determination and self-awareness, and provided a way for disadvantaged constituencies and cultural groups to assert the values of their communities. At other times sport has reproduced the authority of dominant influences, provided opportunities for capitalists motivated mainly by concerns by profit, and underscored and reproduced masculine authority and power even while providing women new opportunities to compete.

In a recent anniversary issue of *Ontario History*, Bruce Kidd makes a spirited case for Ontario's leadership in creating what he calls the Canadian sport system. He acknowledges that Montreal has been generally regarded as the 'cradle of Canadian sport,' but suggests that it was Ontario that promoted the dream of a sporting nation operating along an east–west axis, in opposition to the commercialized blandishments of the American sporting culture. Kidd describes the national leadership of Ontario's athletes, sporting bureaucrats, and journalists and contends that 'the province's place at the heartland of Confederation and the National Policy economy conferred the responsibilities of leadership, obliging them to forge a Canadian sports system and national identities rather than strictly provincial and regional ones.' For Kidd, the story of sportive nation-building is found in how the national sporting federations were established, especially those which promoted the ideals of amateurism. Even though amateurism has given way to professionalized sporting activity in recent years, sport in Canada is still often understood as a way of supporting citizenship and nation building: 'As the heartfelt outpouring of enthusiasm at the time of Olympic, Commonwealth, and other major games indicates, the sports system is arguably the most visible movement for Canadian nationalism today.'

There is little doubt that Ontarians did much to create the national sporting edifice – just as they contributed in many ways to the professionalized, commercialized, and continentalist sporting culture of our own time. Even so, it is important not to ignore the important ways in which sport was being made elsewhere. Sport historians have recently been preoccupied with the processes of ludic diffusion, by which sport radiates outward from the imperial centre to elites in colonial hinterlands and then downward through the social scale. This has tended to emphasize the importance of the metropolis over the hinterland, and to replicate unwittingly the very patterns of imperial dominance and hegemony that imperialists hoped sport would foster. In *Blood, Sweat and Cheers* I have tried to argue that Canada is the product of the lived experience of *all* of us, wherever in this country we live. For that reason it seems important to appreciate the complexity of sporting life, and the struggles engaged in by all who have attempted to make sport conform to their own agendas. Canadian sport history has been made 'on the ground,' so to speak; and in many ways sport in hinterland regions, and among marginalized peoples and ethnic minorities, is as important as that of elite groups in the metropolis. Indeed, the struggles of working people, women, and people of colour to create a more equitable world through sport have been just as important a part of nation building as the creation of sporting organizations, and must be recognized as such. Recreational sporting activity, sport for youth, and alternatives to the dominant Euro-Canadian sporting forms are also part of the story of the making of Canada through sport.

The writing of the history of sport is, like the making of Canada itself, an ongoing and relentless process, always incomplete, always provisional. Although scholarly work over the past two decades has fostered an appreciation of sport's importance to Canadian development, we still need to make our understanding of sport's contribution to national life more inclusive. Much more needs to be done to understand the making of francophone sporting culture, to understand the nature of sport in the North and in Newfoundland, and to elucidate the continuing sporting practices of people in rural communities, which we have largely ignored in our attempts to understand the development of modern organized sport. We still need to know much more about the economic influence that sport has exerted over time, about the complex relationship between sport and gender construction, and about how systems of communication have contributed to national sentiment. We must continue to ponder whether the unifying enthusiasm surrounding sporting events translates into national allegiance over the long term. We need to consider whether sport contributed to the erosion of a socially conscious political culture in Canada in the twentieth century. Much has been done, but much more needs to be done. I hope that *Blood, Sweat, and Cheers* will encourage people to think of these issues, and contribute to the ongoing debate about sport and the making of Canada as we face the challenges of the new century.

Selected Bibliography

Notes on the Sources

The history of sport is a rapidly developing field and involves the long-term contribution of many scholars, most of whom have worked out of departments of physical education and kinesiology. The writing of this book would have not been possible without the substantial contributions they have made over the years. I am indebted in particular to the work of Alan Metcalfe (who read and commented on an earlier draft), Bruce Kidd, Don Morrow, Mark Dyreson, Steve Pope, Morris Mott, Nancy Bouchier, Helen Lenskyj, Vicky Paraschak, Kevin Wamsley, Richard Gruneau, and David Whitson, and to the many members of the North American Society for Sport History, who have made important contributions to our understanding of sport in Canada over the years. Alan Metcalfe's *Canada Learns to Play: The Emergence of Organized Sport, 1807–1914* (Toronto, 1987) is a prodigiously researched book that remains the touchstone for our understanding of sport in Canada before the First World War. I trust that he will understand that my heavy reliance on his work comes from a desire to praise rather than plunder. Bruce Kidd's *The Struggle for Canadian Sport* (Toronto, 1996) focuses on sporting organizations and their role in establishing a national sporting culture, and brings the story into the contemporary period. I rely heavily on his work in my discussions of professionalism, amateurism, and workers' sport associations. Ann Hall, Trevor

Slack, Garry Smith, and David Whitson, *Sport in Canadian Society* (Toronto, 1991) is also indispensable. Donald Guay, *Introduction à l'histoire du sport au Québec* (Montréal, 1987) is the most useful introduction to sport in Quebec – a field that remains largely unresearched. For hockey, Richard Gruneau and David Whitson, *Hockey Night in Canada: Sport, Identities and Cultural Politics* (Toronto, 1993) is the place to start. Two early collections of essays on sport history, Morris Mott, *Sports in Canada. Historical Readings* (Toronto, 1989) and Don Morrow, Mary Keyes, Wayne Simpson, Frank Cosentino, and Ron Lappage, *A Concise History of Sport in Canada* (Toronto, 1989) are essential reference works. So are the many pioneering dissertations that came out of the University of Alberta a few decades ago, especially those of Peter Lindsay, Ron Lappage, Alan Cox, Kevin Jones, Keith Lansley, and Frank Cosentino. Finally, Varda Burstyn's *The Rites of Men: Manhood, Politics, and the Culture of Sport* (Toronto, 1999) is a highly provocative analysis of sport and the production of hegemonic masculinity, although it does not confine itself to the Canadian scene.

Introduction: The Field

Booth, Douglas. 'Swimming, Surfing and Surf-Lifesaving.' In Wray Vamplew and Brian Stoddart, eds., *Sport in Australia: A Social History*. Cambridge, 1984

Burstyn, Varda. *The Rites of Men: Manhood, Politics, and the Culture of Sport*. Toronto, 1999

Dyreson, Mark. *Making the American Team: Sport, Culture, and the Olympic Experience*. Urbana and Chicago, 1998

Geertz, Clifford. 'Deep Play: Notes on the Balinese Cockfight.' *Daedalus* (winter 1972): 2–37

Guttmann, Allen. *From Ritual to Record: The Nature of Modern Sports*. New York, 1978

– *Games and Empires: Modern Sports and Cultural Imperialism*. New York, 1994

– *A Whole New Ball Game: An Interpretation of American Sports*. Chapel Hill, NC, 1988

Lenskyj, Helen. *Out of Bounds: Women, Sport and Sexuality.* Toronto, 1986

Mott, Morris, ed. *Sports in Canada: Historical Readings.* Toronto, 1989

Walden, Keith. *Becoming Modern in Toronto: The Industrial Exhibition and the Shaping of Late Victorian Culture.* Toronto, 1997

Wolf, Naomi. *The Beauty Myth.* Toronto, 1991

1: Blood

Benidickson, Jamie. *Idleness, Water, and a Canoe: Reflections on Paddling for Pleasure.* Toronto, 1997

Bradbury, Bettina. 'Pigs, Cows and Boarders: Non-Wage Forms of Survival among Montreal Families, 1861–1891.' *Labour/Le Travail* 14 (1984): 9–46

Cruikshank, Ken, and Nancy B. Bouchier, '"Sportsmen and Pothunters": Environment, Conservation, and Class in the Fishery of Hamilton Harbour, 1858–1914.' *Sport History Review* 28, no. 1 (May 1997): 1–18

DeLottinville, Peter. 'Joe Beef of Montreal: Working Class Culture and the Tavern, 1869–1889.' *Labour/Le Travail* 8/9 (1981–2): 9–40

Eisen, George. 'Games and Sporting Diversion of the North American Indians as Reflected in American Historical Writings of the Sixteenth and Seventeenth Centuries.' *Canadian Journal of History of Sport and Physical Education* 9, no. 1 (May 1978): 58–85

Howell, Colin, and Christopher Fletcher. 'Modernization Theory and the Traditional Sporting Practices of Native People in Eastern Canada.' *JCPES* 19 (1997): 79–84

Jasen, Patricia. *Wild Things: Nature, Culture, and Tourism in Ontario, 1790–1914.* Toronto, 1995

LeCompte, Mary Lou. *Cowgirls of the Rodeo: Pioneer Professional Athletes.* Urbana, IL, 1993

– 'Cowgirls at the Crossroads: Women in Professional Rodeo, 1885–1922.' *Journal of Sport History* 20, no. 2 (Dec. 1989): 27–48

MacKenzie, John M. *The Empire of Nature: Hunting, Conservation and British Imperialism.* Manchester and New York, 1988

Malcolmson, Robert. *Popular Recreations in English Society, 1700–1850.* Cambridge, 1973

Manning, Richard P. 'Recreating Man: Hunting and Angling in Victorian Canada.' Unpublished MA thesis, Carleton University, 1994

Metcalfe, Alan. *Canada Learns to Play: The Emergence of Organized Sport, 1807–1914.* Toronto, 1987

Pinto-Green, Barbara. 'Charles Wesley Dickinson: A Case Study of a Canadian Cocker, 1860–1914.' North American Society for Sport History, *Proceedings* (1996): 29–30

Rush, Laurie. 'Water Sports and Social Class in the Late Nineteenth Century: A Look at the St. Lawrence Skiff in the Thousand Islands of the St. Lawrence River.' North American Society for Sport History, *Proceedings* (1992): 44–5

Salter, Michael A. 'The Effect of Acculturation on the Game of Lacrosse and on Its Role as an Agent of Indian Survival.' *Canadian Journal of History of Sport and Physical Education* 3, no. 2 (May 1972): 28–43

Tranter, Neil. *Sport, Economy and Society in Britain, 1750–1914.* Cambridge, 1998

Wamsley, Kevin. 'Good Clean Sport and a Deer Apicce: Game Legislation and State Formation in 19th Century Canada.' *Canadian Journal of History of Sport* 25, no. 2 (Dec. 1994): 1–20

Wetherell, Donald G., with Irene Kmet. *Useful Pleasures: The Shaping of Leisure in Alberta, 1896–1945.* Regina, 1990

2: Respectability

Baker, William J. 'Disputed Diamonds: The YMCA Debate over Baseball in the Late 19th Century.' *Journal of Sport History* 19, no. 3 (winter 1992): 257–62

Barman, Jean. *Growing up British in British Columbia: Boys in Private School.* Vancouver, 1984

Bouchier, Nancy. '"Aristocrats" and Their "Noble Sport": Woodstock Officers and Cricket during the Rebellion Era.'

Canadian Journal of History of Sport 20, no. 1 (May 1989): 16–32
- 'Idealized Middle-Class Sport for a Young Nation: Lacrosse in Nineteenth Century Ontario Towns, 1871–1891.' *Journal of Canadian Studies* 29, no. 2 (summer 1994): 89–110
- '"The 24th of May is the Queen's Birthday": Civic Holidays and the Rise of Amateurism in Nineteenth-Century Canadian Towns.' *International Journal of the History of Sport* 10 (1993): 159–92
Bouchier, Nancy, and Robert Barney. 'A Critical Examination of a Source on Early Ontario Baseball: The Reminiscence of Adam E. Ford.' *Journal of Sport History* 15, no. 1 (Spring 1988): 75–90
Brown, David. 'Athleticism and Selected Private Schools in Canada.' Unpublished PhD dissertation, University of Alberta, 1984
Cooper, David. 'Canadians Declare "It Isn't Cricket": A Century of Rejection of the Imperial Game.' *Journal of Sport History* 26, no. 1 (spring, 1999): 51–81
Guttman, Allen. *Games and Empires.* New York, 1994
Howell, Colin. *Northern Sandlots: A Social History of Maritime Baseball.* Toronto, 1995
Howell, David, and Peter Lindsay. 'Social Gospel and the Young Boy Problem 1895–1925.' *Canadian Journal of History of Sport* 17, no. 1 (May 1986): 75–87
Humber, William. *Diamonds of the North: A Concise History of Baseball in Canada.* Toronto, 1995
Kidd, Bruce. *The Struggle for Canadian Sport.* Toronto, 1996
Kidd, Bruce, and John Macfarlane. *The Death of Hockey.* Toronto, 1972
Kossuth, Robert. 'The Rise of Canadian Football and the Decline of English Rugby in Halifax, 1930–1954.' North American Society for Sport History, *Proceedings* (1996): 32–3
Mangan, J.A. *The Games Ethic and Imperialism.* Harmonds-worth, 1986
- 'Muscular, Militaristic, and Manly: The British Middle-Class Hero as Moral Messenger.' *International Journal of the History of Sport* 13, no. 1 (March 1996): 28–47

Marks, Lynne. *Revivals and Roller Rinks: Religion, Leisure and Identity in Late-Nineteenth-Century Small Towns.* Toronto, 1996

McLeod, David I. *Building Character in the American Boy: The Boy Scouts, YMCA, and Their Forerunners, 1870–1920.* Madison, WI, 1983

Metcalfe, Alan. 'A Case Study of Lacrosse.' In Alan Metcalfe, ed., *Canada Learns to Play: The Emergence of Organized Sport, 1807–1914,* 181–218. Toronto, 1987

– 'The Organization of Organized Physical Recreation in Montreal, 1840–1895.' *Social History/Histoire sociale* 11, no. 21 (May 1978): 144–66

– 'Power: A Case Study of the Ontario Hockey Association, 1890–1936.' *Journal of Sport History* 19, no. 1 (spring 1992): 5–25

Morrow, Don. 'Lacrosse as the National Game.' In Don Morrow et al., eds., *A Concise History of Sport in Canada,* 45–68. Toronto, 1989

Palmer, Bryan D. *A Culture in Conflict: Skilled Workers and Industrial Capitalism in Hamilton, Ontario, 1860–1914.* Montreal, 1979

Scobey, David. 'Anatomy of the Promenade: The Politics of Bourgeois Sociability in Nineteenth-Century New York.' *Journal of Social History* 17 (May 1992): 203–277

Vaughan, Garth. *The Puck Starts Here: The Origin of Canada's Great Winter Game, Ice Hockey.* Fredericton, 1996

Wyse, S.F. 'Sport and Class Values in Old Ontario and Quebec.' In Morris Mott, ed., *Sports in Canada: Historical Readings,* 107–29. Toronto, 1989

Young, A.J. 'Sandy'. *Beyond Heroes: A Sport History of Nova Scotia.* 2 vols. Hantsport, NS, 1988

Ziniuk, Dan. 'L'équipe de Denis Boucher.' In William Humber and John St James, eds., *All I Ever Thought about Was Baseball,* 327–32. Toronto, 1996

3: Money

Brown, Douglas A. 'Thoroughbred Horse-Racing Receives an Imperialist Nod: The Parliamentary Debate on Legalizing

Gambling in Canada, 1910.' *International Journal of the History
of Sport* 11, no. 2 (1994): 252–69

Clawson, Mary Ann. *Constructing Brotherhood: Class, Gender, and
Fraternalism.* Princeton, 1989

Cosentino, Frank. *Afros, Aboriginals and Amateur Sport in Pre-
World War One Canada.* Canada Ethnic Group Series, booklet
26, Canadian Historical Association, Ottawa, 1998

Cruise, David, and Alison Griffiths. *Net Worth: Exploding the
Myths of Pro Hockey.* Toronto, 1991

Dyreson, Mark. 'The Emergence of Consumer Culture and
the Transformation of Physical Culture: American Sport in
the 1920s.' *Journal of Sport History* 15, no. 3 (winter 1989):
261–81

Goldstein, Warren. *Playing for Keeps: A History of Early Baseball.*
Ithaca, NY, 1989

Goodman, Jeffrey. *Huddling Up: The Inside Story of the Canadian
Football League.* Don Mills, ON, 1981

Gorn, Eliot J. *The Manly Art: Bare-Knuckle Prize Fighting in
America.* Ithaca, NY, 1986

Joyce, Tony. 'Sport and the Cash Nexus in Nineteenth Century
Canada.' *Sport History Review* 30, no. 2 (Nov. 1999): 140–67

Kidd, Bruce. *Struggle for Canadian Sport,* ch 1–2, 4. Toronto,
1996

Mason, Daniel S. 'The International Hockey League and the
Professionalization of Ice Hockey, 1904–1907.' *Journal of
Sport History* 25, no. 1 (spring 1998): 1–17

McKibbin, Ross. 'Working Class Gambling in Britain, 1880–
1939.' *Past and Present* 82 (1979): 144–78

Morrow, Don. 'A Case Study in Amateur Conflict: The Athletic
War in Canada, 1906–8.' In Morris Mott, ed., *Sports in
Canada: Historical Readings,* 201–19. Toronto, 1989

Morton, Suzanne. *At Odds: Gambling, Regulation and Moral
Ambivalence in Canada, 1919–1969.* (forthcoming)

Peiss, Kathy. *Cheap Amusements. Working Women and Leisure in
Turn-of-the-Century New York.* Philadelphia, 1986

Rozensweig, Roy. *Eight Hours for What We Will: Workers and
Leisure in an Industrial City.* London, 1983

Silver, Jim. *Thin Ice: Money Politics, and the Demise of an NHL Franchise.* Halifax, 1996

Stebbins, Robert A. *Canadian Football: The View from the Helmet.* London, ON, 1987

Vampley, Wray. *Pay up and Play the Game: Professional Sport in Britain.* Cambridge, 1988

Voisey, Paul. Vulcan: *The Making of a Prairie Community.* Toronto, 1988

4: Cheers

Christie, Todd. 'The Eddie Shore – Ace Bailey Incident of 1933: One of the Greatest Tragedies in Canadian Sports History.' *Canadian Journal of History of Sport* 19, no. 1 (May 1988): 63–76

Cosentino, Frank. *Canadian Football: The Grey Cup Years.* Toronto, 1969

Dryden, Ken. *The Game: A Thoughtful and Provocative Look at a Life in Hockey.* Toronto, 1983

Dunning, Eric, and Chris Rojek. *Sport and Leisure in the Civilizing Process: Critique and Counter-Critique.* Toronto, 1992

Elias, Norbert, and Eric Dunning. *Quest for Excitement: Sport and Leisure in the Civilizing Process.* London, 1986

Goldstein, Warren. *Playing for Keeps: A History of Early Baseball.* Ithaca, NY, 1989

Gruneau, Richard, and David Whitson. *Hockey Night in Canada: Sport, Identities and Cultural Politics.* Toronto, 1993

Guttmann, Allen. *Sports Spectators.* New York, 1986

Hoch, Paul. *Rip Off: The Big Game.* Garden City, NY, 1972

Kidd, Bruce and John Macfarlane. *The Death of Hockey.* Toronto, 1972

Lasch, Christopher. 'The Degradation of Sport.' In *The Culture of Narcissism,* ch. 6. Boston, 1984

Lorentz, Stacy L. '"Bowing down to Babe Ruth": Major League Baseball and Canadian Popular Culture.' *Canadian Journal of History of Sport* 26, no. 1 (May 1995): 22–39

Morrow, Don. 'The Myth of the Hero in Canadian Sport
    History.' *Canadian Journal of History of Sport* 23 no. 2 (Dec.
    1992): 72–83
– '"With Craft and Guile": Canada's Jimmy McLarnin and the
    Business of Welterweight Boxing during the Great Depression.'
    Canadian Journal of History of Sport 26, no. 1 (May 1995): 40–51
Nash, Roderick. *The Nervous Generation in American Thought,
    1917–1930*. Chicago, 1970
Rader, Ben. *In Its Own Image: How Television Has Transformed
    Sport*. New York, 1984

5: **Bodies**

Booth, Douglas, and John Loy. 'Sport, Status, and Style.' *Sport
    History Review* 30, no. 1 (May 1999): 1–27
Burstyn, Varda. *The Rites of Men: Manhood, Politics, and the
    Culture of Sport*. Toronto, 1999
Cahn, Susan K. *Coming on Strong: Gender and Sexuality in Twenti-
    eth-Century Women's Sport*. Toronto, 1994
– 'Crushes, Competition, and Closets: The Emergence of
    Homophobia in Women's Physical Education.' In Susan
    Birrell and Cheryl L. Cole, eds., *Women, Sport and Culture*,
    327–40. Champaign, IL, 1994
Cochrane, Jean, Abby Hoffman, and Pat Kincaid. *Women in
    Canadian Life: Sports*. Toronto, 1977
Cruikshank, Ken, and Nancy B. Bouchier. 'Dirty Spaces: Envi-
    ronment, the State, and Recreational Swimming in Hamilton
    Harbour, 1870–1946.' *Sport History Review* 29, no. 1 (May
    1998): 59–76
de Beauvoir, Simone. *The Second Sex*. New York, 1962
Forbes, E.R. 'Battles in Another War: Edith Archibald and the
    Halifax Feminist Movement.' In *Challenging the Regional
    Stereotype*, 67–89. Fredericton, 1989
Gurney, Helen. *A Century to Remember, 1893–1993: Women's Sport
    at the University of Toronto*. Toronto, 1993
Guttmann, Allen. *Women's Sports: A History*. New York, 1991

Hall, M. Ann, and Dorothy A. Richardson. *Fair Ball: Toward Sex Equality in Canadian Sport*. Ottawa, 1982

Kidd, Bruce. 'The Men's Cultural Centre: Sports and the Dynamic of Women's Oppression/Men's Repression.' In Michael A. Messner and Donald F. Sabo, eds. *Sport, Men and the Gender Order: Critical Feminist Perspectives*, ch. 4. Champaign, IL, 1990

– 'Girls' Sports Run by Girls.' Chapter 3 in *The Struggle for Canadian Sport*. Toronto, 1996

Lenskyj, Helen. *Out of Bounds: Women, Sport and Sexuality*. Toronto, 1986

Levy, Joseph, Danny Rosenberg, and Avi Hyman. 'Fanny "Bobbie" Rosenfeld: Canada's Woman Athlete of the Half Century.' *Journal of Sport History*, 26, no. 2 (summer 1999): 392–6

Lorentz, Stacy L. 'Local Teams in a "World of Sport": Sports Coverage and Community Identity in Canadian Daily Newspapers, 1850–1900.' Unpublished paper presented to the North American Society for Sport History, Banff, Alberta. May, 2000

McCrone, Kathleen E. *Playing the Game: Sport and the Physical Emancipation of English Women, 1870–1914*. Lexington, 1988

McKay, Jim. *Managing Gender: Affirmative Action and Organizational Power in Australian, Canadian and New Zealand Sport*. Albany, 1997

Messner, Michael A., and Donald F. Sabo. 'Introduction: Toward a Critical Feminist Reappraisal of Sport, Men and the Gender Order.' In *Sport, Men and the Gender Order: Critical Feminist Perspectives*. Champaign, IL, 1990

Mitchinson, Wendy. *The Nature of Their Bodies: Women and Their Doctors in Victorian Canada*. Toronto, 1991

Prentice, Allison, Paula Bourne, Gail Cuthbert Brandt, Beth Light, Wendy Mitchinson, and Naomi Black. *Canadian Women: A History*. Toronto, 1996

Robinson, Laura. *She Shoots, She Scores: Canadian Perspectives on Women and Sport*. Toronto, 1997

Smith, Michael J. '"Graceful Athleticism or Robust Womanhood": The Sporting Culture of Women in Victorian Nova
Scotia.' *Journal of Canadian Studies* 23, no. 1/2 (spring/
summer 1988): 120–37

Vertinsky, Patricia. *The Eternally Wounded Woman': Women, Doctors
and Exercise in the Late Nineteenth Century*. Manchester, 1990

Wise, S.F., and Douglas Fisher. *Canada's Sporting Heroes*. Don
Mills, ON, 1974

6: Nation

Bumsted, J.M. *The Peoples of Canada: A Post-Confederation History*.
Toronto, 1992

Crocker, J.H. *Report of the Athletic Team at the 1908 Olympic
Games*. Toronto, 1908

Forsyth, Janice. '"Native to Native": Canadian Assimilation
Policy and the Emergence of Indigenous Games.' Unpub-
lished paper presented to the North American Society for
Sport History, Banff, Alberta. May, 2000

Harvey, Jean, and Roger Proulx. 'Sport and the State in Canada.'
In Jean Harvey and Hart Cantelon, eds., *Not Just a Game:
Essays in Canadian Sport Sociology*, 93–120. Ottawa, 1988

Keyes, M. 'Government Involvement in Fitness and Amateur
Sport.' In Don Morrow et. al., eds., *A Concise History of Sport in
Canada*, 256–86. Toronto, 1989.

Kidd, Bruce. 'Canadian Opposition to the 1936 Olympics in
Germany.' *Canadian Journal of History of Sport and Physical
Education* 9, no. 2 (Dec. 1979): 20–40

– 'The Culture Wars of the Montreal Olympics.' *International
Review for the Sociology of Sport* 27, no. 2 (1992): 151–64

– 'The First COA Presidents.' *Olympika: The International Journal
of Olympic Studies* 3 (1994): 107–10

– 'Montreal 1976: The Games of the XXth Olympiad.' In
John E. Findling and Kimberly D. Pelle, eds., *Historical
Dictionary of the Modern Olympic Movement*, 153–60. Westport,
CT, 1996

- 'Ontario and the Ambition of Canadian Sport.' *Ontario History*
  40, no. 2 (1998): 157–72
- 'The Toronto Olympic Commitment: Towards Social Con-
  tract for the Olympic Games.' *Olympika: The International
  Journal of Olympic Studies* 1 (1992): 154–67
Lansley, Keith. 'The AAU and Changing Concepts of Amateur-
  ism.' Unpublished MA thesis, University of Alberta, 1971
Lenskyj, Helen. 'When Winners Are Losers: Toronto and
  Sydney Bids for the Summer Olympics.' *Journal of Sport and
  Social Issues* 20, no. 4 (Nov. 1996): 392–410
MacDonald, Robb. 'The Battle of Port Arthur: A War of Words
  and Ideologies in the Canadian Olympic Committee.' In
  Robert Barney, and Klaus Meyer, eds., *Proceedings: First
  International Symposium for Olympic Research*, 135–52. London,
  ON, 1992
Mallon, William. *The Golden Book of the Olympic Games*. Milan,
  1992
Morrow, Don. 'Grace without Pressure: Canadian Scintillation
  and the Media in the Amsterdam Olympic Games.' In Barney
  and Meier, eds., *Proceedings: First International Symposium for
  Olympic Research*, 125–34. London, ON, 1992
Paraschak, Victoria. 'The Native Sport and Recreation Program,
  1972–1991: Patterns of Resistance, Patterns of Reproduc-
  tion.' *Canadian Journal of History of Sport* 26, no. 2 (Dec.
  1995): 1–18
- '"Recreation North": Continuity and Change, 1967–2000.'
  Unpublished paper presented to the North American Society
  of Sport History conference, Banff, Alberta. May, 2000
Pope, S.W. *Patriotic Games: Sporting Traditions in the American
  Imagination, 1876–1926*. New York, 1997
Roxborough, Henry. *Canada at the Olympics*. 3rd ed. Toronto,
  1973
Stidwell, Howard. 'The History of the Canadian Olympic
  Association.' Unpublished MA thesis, University of Ottawa,
  1982
Wamsley, Kevin. 'Calgary 1988: XVth Olympic Winter Games.'
  In Findling and Pelle, eds., *Historical Dictionary of the Modern
  Olympic Movement*, 310–17. Westport, CT, 1996

Index

THEMES IN CANADIAN SOCIAL HISTORY

Editors:
Craig Heron 1997–
Franca Iacovetta 1997–1999